GET THE POOP OUT OF YOUR NAILS

AND OTHER WAYS TO ENJOY MOTHERHOOD

CHRISTY JOCEK

Print ISBN: 978-1-09833-587-8

eBook ISBN: 978-1-09834-062-9

CONTENTS

DEDICATION

To Olivia, who made me a mom, and I couldn't be happier about that. To Riley, who made me a boy mom, which is more fun than I ever imagined. And to Madelyn, who completed our family is such a fantastic way. I love you three with everything in me.

CHAPTER ONE

LET'S GET ACQUAINTED

When you hear the word *mom* what word comes to mind? Do you picture your mother? Maybe a famous TV mom? Does the image of an older woman wearing elastic waist jeans pop into your mind? We all have an idea of who *Mom* is—what she does, what she wears, and how she looks. But when you call up this idea in your mind, do you think of yourself? Do you easily roll yourself into the image of *mom*, or are you still too unsure of yourself? Still not confident in this role of yours? Still feel like you just might not measure up? I hope not.

I hope you are settling into motherhood. I hope you are feeling capable and strong in this extremely overwhelming role. I would love to know that you feel as though you are thriving, but if I had to guess, you don't. You doubt yourself, you are too hard on yourself, and motherhood just might not be what you envisioned. If that is you, stay with me. These pages are here to encourage you and build you up. I will never pretend it's easy, or that I have all the answers, but I have been there, still am here, and I understand. I want to give you practical, tangible advice, as well as the freedom to be you and the kind of mom you want to be; whether you birthed your kids, adopted your kids, or married into your kids, I am all about experiencing a happy motherhood.

So what comes next? What's this book all about? It's about motherhood; it's *not* a parenting book. It's for and about moms. Moms are the bedrock of every civilization and every community. I want to celebrate that and be real about it too. We need to be able to examine motherhood and all of its complexities, and just be open and honest about it. In my twenty years of being a mom, I've come to understand certain things a little differently than I did in the beginning of motherhood. My guess is that you are all about making a wonderful childhood for your kids. You want to be all in and your goal is to raise great people. But I'm also guessing you haven't factored in your own feelings. You haven't thought about being intentional in making a wonderful motherhood for yourself. So, while your heart is for your kids—mine is for you! My goal is to dive into everything motherhood in an attempt to guide you in your journey of being a mother.

Additionally, this book, which celebrates mothers, is not a critique of fathers. It's not a chance to tear down the men in our lives, or blame them for our issues. If that's the space you're in, you need a different book! Fatherhood is so important and critical, and I don't want to downplay its importance. For now, though, we're just talking woman to woman.

My goal is not to sway you to a specific side of a particular subject. I am not going to preach about breastfeeding versus bottle-feeding, working full time versus staying at home, or when to get your toddler to give up the pacifier already! I'm not a fan of the argumentative nature our culture has taken on. We seem to think everyone has to agree on every single issue and idea. All I care about is if you are a mom. I don't care if you gave birth naturally, ate your placenta, or breastfeed your eight year old (OK, maybe that one!). My point is motherhood is hard enough. We need to support one another. We don't have to parent the same way or agree on *all* the things.

We will also explore the dreaded *mom guilt* a lot in these chapters. I believe mom guilt reigns supreme over all other kinds of guilt. You may say it's the *mother* of all guilt. Moms have put such an insane amount of pressure on themselves to be everything and everyone to their little ones. And the more kids they have, the guilt just grows. It comes from a loving heart, but it has dire consequences. It's the biggest destroyer of enjoying motherhood, and the hardest mindset to break.

So, this book is all about you, Mom! My desire for you is to not just survive motherhood, but to thrive in it. I want you to actually enjoy being a mom. Motherhood is hard. It's messy. It's unpredictable and it's exhausting. However, there are currently over 43 million of us. That is because it's also the most wonderful, thrilling and fulfilling thing you'll ever do. You are not going to enjoy every day as a mom; you will make mistakes and question yourself repeatedly. But, through all of that, the good and the bad, I strongly believe that all moms can succeed in motherhood. Moms should look back and not just see the great childhood they created for their kids, but the great *motherhood* they created for themselves too. I want them to feel that they didn't just raise kids, but that they grew as well, and flourished in a role that was bigger than anything else they ever did—and hopefully were able to enjoy it along the way.

* * *

My journey to motherhood was pretty straightforward, quite honestly. My husband Mike and I had been working with a non-profit organization straight out of college. A few years in we decided to move on and start a new focus. He got into IT and I got into baby fever. The only other job I wanted was *Mommy*. So we decided to start trying, and bam, first month—pregnant! I hadn't expected it to work so fast, but there I was staring at the plus sign on a stick! It was quite shocking, really. So after leaving a life we thought we were sure of, Mike got a new job, we bought a house, and I got pregnant. All in one month's time. It was exciting and scary, and quite a whirlwind to say the least.

I truly wish I could say I loved being pregnant—that I glowed and nested. But I did not. I don't know who coined the phrase "morning sickness," because it should be called "all-the-live-long-day-sickness!" That was me. I was getting sick about seven or eight times a day, so my introduction to motherhood left a lot to be desired! It wasn't fun, and it definitely wasn't pretty. I pushed through as best I could, though (while keeping a bucket with me at all times!). It was a great first lesson in motherhood. It's all about giving of yourself for someone else, being selfless and readjusting expectations. Welcome to being a mom, right?

So here's my first piece of advice to moms—yes it starts in utero. Don't feel guilty if you are not one of the darling, glowing pregnant ladies. You may be one of the sweaty, bloated, ankles-the-size-of-your-thighs pregnant ladies. It will have absolutely no bearing on you as a mom. If anything, you will be a better mom for it because you'll be so happy to get that baby out! I am only 5'2'' with a short torso, so my pregnant body wasn't even close to darling. Pregnancy truly took over my whole body, not just my belly. Even my nose grew!

Our first baby was born in early 2000. Besides being sick constantly, everything had been going just fine. I was measuring low on amniotic fluid, so that last week my doctor had me lie down after meals and count baby movements. As long as there were ten in an hour's time, all was well. I had been doing that, getting 25-30 movements before an hour was even up. Then one morning, four days after my due date, and after forgetting to do it the night before, I laid down after breakfast to count. *I had two movements in an hour.* Frantic, I called my doctor's office and they said to come in right away. After hooking me up to the fetal heart monitor they told me to head straight to the hospital—the baby was basically out of fluid and needed to come out.

And there was my first experience with mommy guilt. This baby hadn't even been born yet, and I already felt I failed it by forgetting to count movements the night before. What if my forgetfulness caused a problem or irreversible damage? Thankfully, Mike was with me and we got to the hospital fast. Once there, they broke my water and nothing came out. I was completely dry. It was super scary and overwhelming, but by that night we had our beautiful, healthy baby girl, Olivia. She was absolutely fine and we were beyond grateful.

We didn't find out ahead of time what we were having. I pretended to not care, but...I cared. I wanted a girl badly. Maybe I should feel some kind of prescribed mom guilt over this, but I don't. (No need for you to either!) So when I delivered this little squirmy thing and they said, "It's a girl!" I was kind of shocked. We had conceived so easily, I thought surely God wouldn't let me have a girl too! I don't know where I picked up that kind of silly logic, but somehow I did.

When Olivia came into our lives, I was gob smacked. There is no other word to use here. I had wanted a baby badly, but I never, ever expected to fall so hard in love like I did. It did me in. I was enthralled by every little inch of her little cute body and every little sigh out of her mouth. She quickly became my world (hence, my need for a book like this). I just had no way to anticipate the depth of love I would feel as a mother.

I was a stay-at-home-mom from the start. Thankfully, I had a very supportive husband who was in favor of it. I will share much more about my foray into staying at home in another chapter, but I will tell you, staying at home was a lot harder than I expected. I can't say I loved it. I don't think I had postpartum depression; I think I had staying-at-home-depression. When I became a mom, this was not a term or condition anyone talked about, but it is exactly how I felt. Becoming a stay-at-home mom was a rough transition—I thought I would love it, and then didn't. It had nothing to do with becoming a mom because I enjoyed that immensely. But being alone all day without adult interaction was hard on me and I didn't enjoy being stuck in the house, or at least feeling like I was. I hadn't expected to feel a "lesser than" mentality around other women either. Then knowing how many moms would love to be in my position added to my angst because I knew it was a privilege—I just wanted to enjoy it more. It felt like a giant letdown because it was supposed to be wonderful and magical, like I had imagined, but it clearly wasn't. And then came the guilt over not loving it, and a whole vicious cycle began.

The first two weeks of her life Olivia was "failing to thrive." Breastfeeding was super difficult; she wasn't gaining any weight and had gone days without pooping. So an immerging hard and stressful situation became pretty serious, pretty fast. After a second visit to a lactation consultant we realized Olivia's tongue was preventing her from sucking correctly. The lactation consultant weighed her, had me nurse, and then weighed her again. I thought it was one of our better times and was frustrated that it had happened so easily while in the office. But after weighing her, it turned out she only had gotten 1/16th of an ounce. I was shocked. And you can imagine the other feeling that crept in—guilt. In my mind I had been starving my baby and should have realized. Our pediatrician said we had to supplement with a bottle, which we promptly did. I don't know why she could suck fine from a bottle and not from me, but I didn't have time to agonize over it. I was just glad she could. I pumped every bottle for her until about six months in when I couldn't take it anymore. Mike jokingly referred to me as "Bessie," yes, as in the cow, because I was pumping a good 16 ounces of milk from each side every morning! Nothing's sexier than that, right ladies?

After several months I started making strides and life was going more smoothly...then, bam! Pregnant again. Our son Riley arrived 18 months after Olivia. My pregnancy with him was much easier. I still got sick, but not quite as often. It was much harder to deal with though, because Olivia was still so young at the time and needed so much of my attention. I do have a clear memory of hovering over the toilet and Mike asking if there was anything he could do. I glared at him and said, "Yeah, you can pray this is a boy because I am NOT doing this again!" Pretty loving, right? It's ironic because it was a boy, but spoiler alert, I did do it again!

I started having amniotic fluid issues again with Riley, so my doctor was keeping closer tabs this time around. Three weeks before his due date, it was confirmed that I was leaking fluid, and they said he needed to be born. They induced me and seven hours later Riley entered the world. There was some concern over him since he was early, but he was completely healthy and did great. We knew this time around that we were having a boy. It was fun having both experiences of knowing and not knowing the gender. I think either way it's a surprise, it's just about how soon you want to know it.

Life was instantly changed again. You think the second time should be easier. You know what to expect, you are surer of yourself, you have a routine. Well that may be true, but the first time you didn't have a toddler hanging on you while you figured it all out! I didn't find it easier at all. So, if you are in this spot right now, just know it's OK. It's OK if things are hard, if you have to give your first born more attention than the baby, and if you haven't bonded as fast the second time around. It takes time to acclimate after having a baby. It doesn't always happen naturally or easily. I didn't give myself that grace and I really wish I had. We moms can be so unnecessarily hard on ourselves.

Clearly I got through it, because two and a half years after Riley, our daughter Madelyn was born. I also had to be induced with her because of fluid issues, this time just one week early. Four hours and only two pushes later (thank you, Jesus), she came out and completed our family.

Three babies in four years' time. Life wasn't just changed, it was crazy. To be sure, there was not a whole lot of thriving going on! I was absolutely in survival mode. I can even remember a few times begging Mike not to go to work and "leave me with these people." Madelyn was my easiest pregnancy and delivery, but my hardest toddler. She had a wild streak like I hadn't seen before. The stories we have about her are legendary—public tantrums, Sharpie art on a brand new couch, and a getting lost in Kohl's incident that aroused a panic in me I had never known before. I was at the checkout and looked away for three seconds and she was gone. I couldn't find her anywhere. I've never known terror like I did that day. After they completely locked down the store and I went running and screaming like a lunatic for her, an employee found her sitting under a display of clothes. After my tearful reunion I wanted to make sure she was OK through that traumatizing experience, but all she said was that she was "scared of dinosaurs." Right. She was just fine! Thankfully, her orneriness eased out of her by elementary school and she is now one of the most laid-back people I know. But it made for a very challenging few years.

Let me just say now, each stage of motherhood is hard. Each stage is different. Just as your kids will go through stages, so will you as a mom. I am not the same mom in 2020 as I was in 2000. And I thank God for that. Each stage gets easier, and then it gets harder (I'm talking to you, teenage years!). The wonderful thing is, as your kids grow and mature, you will too. Your job is to settle in. Enjoy it as it happens. I think too many moms forget to enjoy it. Their focus is on getting everyone fed, clothed and not too dirty that they can't go to Target. Or, well maybe to Walmart. I want moms to ditch guilt and embrace the journey. My goal is to give you tips on how to do just that.

You'll also hear from some of my mom friends—women I have walked with through motherhood and whom I've had the privilege of seeing thrive. I sent out questions to a dozen or so of my friends whose opinions I value. I expected to get a ton of great material to work with—lots of interesting views and thoughts. The exact opposite happened. Almost everyone said a variation of the same types of things. At first I was disappointed, worried that I hadn't received a good enough variety. But soon I realized it only confirmed that I had obtained a lot of truth. If every mom I questioned is saying the same things, then I know I'm on to something. And that something is what we all craved to hear as young moms ourselves. It's exciting to pass it all to the next generation of new moms.

You'll get a few hilarious quotes and lots of stories thrown in too, because sometimes all you can do as a mom is laugh at the craziness of it all!

"I've been both a working mom and a stay—at— home mom. In both scenarios I say to pay attention/ be observant of your child/children. Watch for good and bad changes in their behavior. Notice and encourage their gifts and talents. Sometimes things have to change for the betterment of the family."

Rory from Ohio

Booty Call: a shout from the bathroom letting you know it's time to go wipe someone's butt.

@babyhellfire

"It's spicy." – Universal mom code for "I don't want to share."

HMJonesWriter

Just because they don't sleep during nap time doesn't mean you stop doing it. Make them rest or look at books. Kids need rest time and you need the quiet time.

Melissa from Ohio

CHAPTER TWO

TWO AREAS TO DISCUSS

First things first, before diving in any further, there are two topics I want to address. There are mindsets I see moms take on that set them up for failure, often without even knowing it. Or, they might not be out-and-out failing, but they are definitely in the surviving-not-thriving mentality.

So, I am going to put this out there. You may not like me for it, but I think there's so much freedom in it:

You can't have it all. You can't do it all.

What a lie we've bought into! It's not completely our faults; it's been ingrained in us. This lie tells us we can be full-time professionals, full-time mothers, full-time wives, full-time friends, sisters, aunts; you get the picture...all simultaneously, of course, with perfect make-up and cute boots. It's a trap to think you can do all these things, be all these things, all at the same time. And if you don't, you're a failure or less-than. You have to allow yourself the freedom to say *I can't do it all and I don't need to take on that pressure*. There is simply no need.

There is surely someone in your life that you can think of like this. It may very well be you! This woman wants to do it all, and do it well. There is nothing wrong with that desire; however, it just isn't attainable, or sustainable. A balanced work/home life is just plain hard. And if you have more than one kid you know that often times one of them will get less of your time and even attention. It's inevitable sometimes. At some point you must realize that you can have *some* of it all and can do *some* of it all, but life will become so much harder if you are always striving for more and more and more. My advice is to pick what your primary goal is, what your secondary goal is and then work within those parameters. But some things will have to get laid aside. Some relationships may need to take a back seat in your life.

As a side note, you know the group that doesn't seem to believe this lie that they can have it all? Men. Men don't have this kind of insane pressure on them to do it all. I assume this is because historically men were typically in charge of the "outside the home" work, while women did the work inside. When more and more women went into the workforce, unfortunately, they also believed they had to do everything they were already doing, too. It's like, "Fine if you want to be doctors and lawyers, but still have dinner on the table at 5 p.m." You have to give this type of thinking up. It's antiquated for one, but also harmful to you. Take a lesson from the men in your life. If they can't do something, they are more likely to say so. Or they simply don't do it. And while men aren't exactly known for their willingness to ask for help, we all know a man who would benefit from doing so. So will you, moms!

Instead of feeling bitter that no one expects men to balance everything perfectly, why not just reject the idea that women do? Do what you can and leave the rest alone. This doesn't always come naturally for us; it's absolutely a learned behavior. But if you want to enjoy your kids' childhoods, it will be worth learning.

I know I am hammering this point home, and I don't want to sound redundant, but please do not straddle yourself with guilt. I believe so strongly that mom guilt is the single worst enemy to thriving in motherhood. When you allow yourself to not "do it all," there is a freedom from guilt. Whether you are a stay-at-home mom or full-time working mom, it doesn't matter. Every mom will struggle with this at times. If you tell yourself that you alone have to take care of your home, your kids, husband, animals, yard, errands, doctor appointments, the PTO—you will feel overwhelmed. You will lose your joy. You won't thrive. Saying no when you need to, and asking for help when you need it, are two ways you will flourish as a mom.

The other thing to think about with the "you can't do it all" argument is your reasoning for wanting to "do it all." Are you a Type A kind of person who genuinely likes working on making things better, and likes being in the action? There is nothing wrong with that. However, if you are that kind of person, you will think it's up to you, or that you are the only one who can do it well. There aren't enough hours in the day, Mom. You have to lay aside some things, because ultimately your kids and your husband need you. The PTO board will survive a meeting without you. Your co-worker will survive without you at the business social event. You have to learn to prioritize and decide which things are the most important and which things are lower on the list. And maybe, just maybe, realize that other people can handle some of the things! If you don't, you will simply burn out. No one can be at their best when that happens.

Or is your reason settled in proving your self-worth? Maybe you think you have to do it all to prove something to yourself, your husband, your parents, or whomever. Do you feel like taking on more than you need is proof that you are some kind of Super Mom? Because, let me just tell you, she doesn't exist. Don't fall in that trap of chasing after her. It will get you nowhere but exhausted.

When my kids were little, I loved throwing them birthday parties. I didn't go crazy overboard, but I did love to go big with a theme. I put so much pressure on myself to have the creatively-themed food, cute goodie bags and the best decorations. I scoured the internet looking for everything from Star Wars lightsaber pretzel rods to make-your- own Princess tiaras. By the time the party rolled around, I was so exhausted from planning it, that hosting wasn't all that fun. I did want to give my kids fun, memorable parties, but I think part of me was trying to be Super Mom. Was I trying to show that I was an amazing hostess? To a bunch of six-year-olds? Did serving "Yoda Soda" at my son's Star Wars party or serving a fancy tiered cake instead of a sheet cake fill some need in me to feel validated? Silly and a waste of my energy!

Maybe you are trying to make up for what you didn't have growing up. If your mom was not the bake-cookies-after-school mom, didn't seem interested in your life, or was possibly absent altogether; you may be striving to fill a void in yourself. While there is nothing wrong with wanting to make things special for your children, and being involved in their lives is important, there is a danger in doing it for the wrong reasons. We can't create magical Christmases and memorable traditions for our kids in an attempt to heal ourselves from past hurts or unfulfilled needs. Anyone doing special things for the wrong reasons can easily burn out and will most likely end up feeling like a failure—thus, no void gets filled. So, say you love Elf on the Shelf (I will admit I am so glad this did not exist when my kids were small; it seems like just one more way at add stress to the holidays!) or being room mom in your kids' class, or chaperoning field trips—by all means do it! But do it because you love your kids, and maybe even Elf on the Shelf, but not because you need to fill a void in your own life.

Ultimately, you are the only person who can control your schedule and workload. If you want to flourish as a mom, don't put too much on your plate at once. Learn to say no when you need to and don't go on guilt trips. They aren't worth it.

* * *

The Great Debate

So here's the second big issue I feel strongly about:

Can we get over the "Stay-at-Home Mom versus Working Mom" debate? I really don't even understand why there is still an argument over this. This is probably the biggest "mom war" women find themselves in (second is breastfeeding versus bottle feeding, or maybe "natural" birth versus epidurals, or maybe...). This seems to bring out the "mama bear" in us. I think it's partially because it's such a personal decision. We feel strongly about the choice we made, so when someone else makes a different one, we feel threatened and challenged.

But here's the mindset we need to take: If you think staying at home with your kids is best, do it. If you think working full-time while mothering is best, do it. Do not be threatened by someone else's choice—it's theirs, not yours. Because, guess what? If you are doing your best, your kids are going to turn out fine either way. I know so many wonderful kids who were raised by a full-time parent. I know just as many wonderful kids who had full-time working parents. Maybe there's some freedom in knowing you can screw your kid up just as easily whether you are at home or at work?

I have to admit that when I first became a mom, I was very solid in my belief that staying at home was best. I was probably—dare I admit it—prideful about my choice. But a few things changed and humbled me to where I stand now, and I don't feel that way so strongly anymore.

For one, I have a lot more full-time working friends and relatives. They are all great moms. They love their kids just as much as I do. They make up the time and spend solid quality time when they have it. If you think about it, when you have a good 12-14 hours a day every day with your kid, the time is much more about quantity and not always quality. So, who is to say which kid is getting more valuable one-on-one time with their mother?

Secondly, my kids grew up. It's hard to imagine if you are reading this right now and you have a newborn in your arms, but that little baby will grow up. Fast. And they will not need you as much. I remember the day Madelyn, my baby, went to first grade. It was the first time in ten years that I was home all day alone. I kind of looked around and thought, "Huh. Now what?" That whole stay-at-home-mom depression I mentioned earlier came back with a vengeance. I realized that I would need a new focus and direction in my life, or I would easily spiral down.

Now, I am not saying your kids don't need you as they get older—just not as much as they used to. I think all ages, especially teenagers, need Mom and Dad around. They need to feel supported and cared for. But at this point they can wipe their own butt and make a sandwich, thank the Lord. So, while your role is still indispensable, your amount of care isn't. It's easy to feel purposeless at this point. If you haven't done anything leading up to this point to combat it, you will suffer for it.

Another reason my perspective changed on the working versus stay-at-home mom debate came years later also, and is much more practical in nature. After staying home for a number of years, it was challenging to get a "real job" afterwards. It's hard to be a 40-something with a Bachelor's degree but no real work experience. I have had a very hard time trying to get back into what I *wanted to be when I grew up*. It came time to draft a resume and I was at a loss. Somehow, I don't think any executives are going to be impressed by my mommy multi-tasking skills. "Can nurse a baby, read to a toddler, help with fifth grade math, and listen to pre-teen angst all at the same time!" It just won't cut it on a resume. So if your career is important to you, the time you will be away from it is absolutely a factor when making your decision. This was, of course, only my experience. Depending on your education and work history, this will vary a ton for each person.

If this feels true for you too or you are struggling with this choice, my honest opinion and best advice is to contemplate working part-time. I think this could have been a good solution for me and I have wondered what kind of difference it would have made in my motherhood journey. Think about it this way— you get to keep a part of your pre-baby world and you also get to spend a lot of time with the baby. Moms that work part-time can have the best of both worlds, or at least the closest to that as possible. I really wish more companies would do job sharing. I've heard that some companies have started doing this and it just seems like a very practical answer for many people. You get moms and dads who want to stay in the workforce, but also want solid time at home. Why not find two people that can share the 40 hours a week? It works for the parent because they are not stressing about leaving their child full-time, and are even excited to get a break (you can admit it, it's OK). In turn, it makes them work harder and more productively while they are there, so it's a win for the employer as well. I would rather have two fresh faced employees each week than one who is tired and stressed out. And, most likely, the employees have a spouse who works full-time and, thus, they are likely to not need health benefits—another win for the employer. Seems like common sense to me, and a very easy solution to a problem millions of people face every day!

So, no matter what choice you have made since becoming a mom, just remember this: There is no right or wrong here, nor is there a prescription. Every mom is doing what she believes is best and every mom loves her kids fiercely and wants the very best for them. Someone else's approach to work and family might not look the way it looks in your home and that is OK. It's not your home. People today seem to get so tied to their opinions that they have a very hard time letting anyone else have their own. At the end of the day, whatever choice you make, do it well. Do it unapologetically. And don't judge other moms. We should be supporting each other regardless of how many hours we are home during the day.

90% of parenting is thinking about when you can lie down again.

@relaxingmommy

"I think I needed someone to tell me that if the outcome of my parenting didn't match the expectations of my parenting, AND my kids were happy and healthy, I was doing a good job. I struggled for a long time because I grew up wanting to be a stay-at-home mom. Our circumstances didn't allow for this. I felt like I wasn't being a good enough mom because my expectations for parenting were different than my outcome. My kids have been happy and healthy even though I have harbored a lot of guilt about vthis. It's not necessary. As moms, we put way too much pressure on ourselves."

Jenny in Ohio

Motherhood is so exciting because there are so many surprises, like when will I sleep next? How many days in a row can I use dry shampoo? Is it obvious that I'm not wearing a bra? Is anyone even listening to me?!

@belinda.liucci.soakai

CHAPTER THREE

STAY-AT-HOME MOMS

So, you're a stay-at-home mom. Great! I applaud you, I support you and I feel you. Whether you have been at it for one week or ten years, you know it's a hard job. No other job will you work this hard, for well, absolutely nothing. The hours stink and the only way to get a promotion is to give birth again. Oh, but the time together is the biggest reward.

Like I said, it's a hard job. But I have to say something— it's controversial and just might ruffle your feathers...

It's not the hardest job in the world.

Um, did I just say that? I was a stay-at-home mom for 12 years (and am still a part-time one) and I can't tell you how many people, upon hearing my "profession" would comment with, "Oh, that's the hardest job in the world." I have to say I found it extremely disingenuous and even patronizing. It was usually followed with awkward silence and uneasiness. I knew they didn't really mean it and were wondering what I did all day long.

Don't get me wrong, being a stay-at-home mom is absolutely a hard job. It's emotionally challenging and physically demanding to be sure. But let's face it—it's not rocket science or running into burning buildings or treating cancer patients. I mean, you can go to work in your jammies and you have no commute. The only way it's the hardest job is the non-existent paycheck, and I have no solution to that problem, unfortunately!

You see, I think there is a dangerous by-product of staying at home—or I should say in staying at home and seeing it as the "hardest job in the world." It has the potential to turn into a very ugly thing called martyrdom. If you chose to be a stay-at-home mom, own it. Don't become a martyr over it. It is hard, but it can't become a reason to feel sorry for yourself or to feel inferior.

If you feel inferior to working moms, you will undoubtedly fall into the martyrdom mommy trap. You will wish you could wear nice clothes and go on power lunches. You could start resenting your kids, husband, and your very own life. If you feel sorry for yourself, you will become lethargic and won't excel at motherhood. It would be easy to fall into the mentality that everyone has it better than you and you'll start hating your life. Fight this at all costs. Your husband and children will suffer under both of those thought processes, but you will even more. Your mindset will be far from thriving.

As I mentioned earlier, my first years staying home were rough. I struggled with feeling unsure of how to use my time, how much time I needed to spend one-on-one with my kids, how much to spend on my home, and...did this mean my husband was now my boss? Supervisor? I had this weird twisted way of thinking—I felt like I had to tell him everything I did during the day to kind of justify my staying home. He never did anything to make me feel this way, mind you—I somehow conjured that all up myself. He would say, "How was your day?" I would answer, "I cleaned the bathroom and did three loads of laundry."

Don't do this. Unless you really *are* just lying around all day watching Netflix, don't assume that is what anyone else thinks you are doing. You are doing important, valuable work—do not break it down into a list of chores. If you see value in what you are doing, then be proud of it. Work hard; you do need to clean the bathroom, but don't devalue the time you have with your kids. If you were working with someone else's kids you would be a *Childcare Professional*. I don't know why it's different when it's your own kids. You are still investing in kids' lives every day, which is a hugely important role. Being with them more than anyone else is a privilege not to be taken lightly.

* * *

A few months into becoming a mom, I was itching to be around people. I found a Mommy and Me baby music/play group. It was all singing and bouncing and trying to get babies to care about maracas. It was great for Olivia, but I needed more.

I did some research on moms' groups, attended a few, but didn't find any I loved. So, I started a MOPS (Mothers of

Pre-Schoolers) chapter in my town. A few friends joined me and we created this little safe haven. It was truly a lifeline. Take your baby to all the music, tumbling, and story times you want, but invest in you too! Our group was mostly focused on motherhood issues. It was there that I quickly saw the difference between motherhood issues and parenting issues. They aren't the same, but both equally need to be tended to. Parenting issues really are about the child and the family as a whole—anything from establishing bedtimes to when you'll allow your kids to date fall into this category. But motherhood issues are about you and you alone. You are too valuable to not spend time developing who you are as a woman.

You need to find a group, whether it's a formal organization or not. Grab some girlfriends and talk. Then talk some more. Talk about your kids if you want. But discuss everything else too. Everything from religion and politics to your celebrity crush and favorite moisturizer. It's good for your soul. And, believe it or not, it will make you a better mom. You cannot allow your whole world to be about your kids. I get it—your kids are the best, cutest, smartest humans on the planet, right?

But, here's the thing. They leave. They will leave you and if you made them your entire world, then your world will become very empty and meaningless. Your identity cannot be wrapped up in them. So, here is the most important advice I think I can give you...

Give your all to your kids, but don't make them your all.

If you do your job right, they will become independent, thriving adults who will want to make their own mark on the world. Congratulations, Mom, you did your job. You made *your* mark. Then it will be time to find a new one. If you haven't invested any time into anything else, especially yourself, you will feel lonely and purposeless. So, work at it now to avoid that hardship later. Things like mom groups, hobbies, and passionate discussions about the world around you will help fight those feelings. Do anything that keeps you connected to who you are as *you*, not just as Mommy.

Another reason to invest in yourself is that it will make you a better wife. Even if your husband is just as head-over-heels about your kids as you are, he will want to talk about other things! He will want to talk to his wife, not just his kids' mom. You need to have more in your world so that there are many topics to discuss, not just filling him in on who went potty and where. It's also crucial so that when he walks in the door after work you are not so starving for adult conversation that you pounce on him before he even gets through the door. It's not fair to him, or you!

We will talk more about husbands in a coming chapter, but since we are also discussing stay-at-home moms, this is where it really hits home for you. A stay-at-home wife has different issues that will pop up. It could be easy for you to become envious of him. After becoming parents, his life will not change as drastically as yours. I realized this after kids and I became very resentful of Mike. He would talk about work and people and sometimes things that were actually very boring, but I got bitter and jealous. I wanted more stories to tell than what Dora the Explorer was up to that day. That is a very ugly and unhealthy way to live because those feelings only grow bigger and stronger. You can fight it by reminding yourself that yes, it can be hard, but it was also something you chose to do. Getting resentful with your husband over it is unfair to him and counter-productive on many levels. For one, his working full-time is most likely the reason you are able to stay home. He is working so you can stay home and is taking a lot on his shoulders in being the primary breadwinner. To be sure, you are also taking a lot on your shoulders as primary parent. Both are extremely important. But it can't become a competition between the two of you as to who has it harder. It's also unfair because the two of you are getting a very unequal amount of time with your kids. He may feel bitter for the time he is missing out on with the kids, just as much as you are feeling bitter that he gets to be out in the world. Seems like a much healthier way of living if you try to understand each other's side and work at feeling compassionate and supportive towards one another instead.

* * *

Another dangerous feeling that can pop up is unworthiness. I felt this way for years too, until I was able to identify it and intentionally drive it out. I let myself fall into the trap that since I was "just a stay-at-home mom" I wasn't interesting, couldn't be in intellectual conversations, or didn't measure up to the women my husband worked with. You just can't let yourself go there. It is easy to stay in this little mommy bubble when you stay home, but you have to pop it once in a while. Staying at home is something to be proud of, not a reason to feel embarrassed or to look down on yourself. If you feel unworthy, uninteresting, or inferior in any way, it will material-ize in how you present yourself. Don't let it. Watch the news, take a class, stay up to date on the world around you, and you will always have important things to discuss at dinner par-ties (yes, those days will come) or just at home with the hubby. But, ultimately, if you value what you are doing, others will too.

I needed to be reminded of this more than once. I remember being at my kids' elementary school for parent/teacher conferences. It was for my youngest, Madelyn. I was in the hallway waiting my turn and was looking at all the kids' papers the teacher had taped up on the walls. The kids, who were in first grade, had to write a few sentences to answer the question, "What do my parents do?" I scanned all the lined pages looking for Maddie's. When I found it, I didn't know if I should laugh or cry. Her answer to the question was, "My dad fixes computers. My mom shops all day." Wow, way to make a mom feel valued, right? When I asked her about it later, she said she just meant that I do "the grocery shopping and stuff." I'm not sure that did a lot to make me feel better!

* * *

While we are on the subject of feeling unworthy, finances obviously come up. It is silly to pretend this isn't an issue. Ideally, if you've made the stay-at-home choice, you are able to swing it financially. But most likely it has come at a cost. My husband and I have definitely felt the crunch of living on one income and it can absolutely become a source of contention. But I believe any marriage can weather that storm.

My best advice here is to look at the money you are saving by being home. The average childcare costs in America are $972 a month. That amount is staggering to me. And since most families have more than one child, that number can really skyrocket. I always thought that although I wasn't bringing in income, I was saving us from paying out income. With three kids so close together, paying for childcare would have been monumental for us. Keep in mind, if you do go back to work when the kids start school, you'll only be home for a few years, so cutting back for a short period on nonessential things makes living on one income very doable. Again, there is no right answer here. However things work in your family, I simply want you to feel at peace about it.

You need to make sure that if you and your husband have made the choice for you to stay at home, you stand firm together. You make financial decisions together and you make a budget together. Just because he is the "breadwinner" does not mean you don't matter in financial discussions or decisions. It also means that you should be united in how to cut back where necessary and help keep each other accountable in that area. Working on this as a team will obviously help your finances, but it will also help your marriage. You will not feel like you don't have a say or any clout when it comes to your finances, which will hopefully keep more peace in your marriage.

As a side note, another thing to watch for is that ugly green-eyed monster—good old-fashioned jealousy. If you've committed to staying home, it feels good right up to the point when you scroll through Facebook and see a friend's second (or is it third?) vacation post. She is a working mom, and her family is enjoying two salaries. You will have to keep on scrolling, Mom, because staying at home just may mean you get one (or no) vacations. Vacation for you may mean a trip to McDonald's Playland. Do not get tripped up on this. You will not be here forever and extra one-on-one time with your kids is way more valuable, anyway. If you are sure you made the right choice for your family, you can't let someone else's salary or salaries, keep you from fulfilling what you believe is best.

* * *

Don't lose yourself.

This happens easier than you might think. Your world has changed drastically. You have changed, but you are still you. You need to remember who "you" are, just much as you need to learn how to be "mommy." It is extremely easy to lose sight of that when you are so focused on caring for your children. So, here are some really practical ways to not let that happen.

Tip one: Take a shower. Daily. Wash your hair. Weekly? As silly as it sounds, it's an important and pretty basic component in feeling like yourself. I have known too many moms who complain (possibly even brag—it's hard to decipher sometimes) about how they can't get a shower. There is either no time or the baby "won't let them." That's the one that really gets me—the baby won't let you? Has the baby turned into a 300 pound sumo wrestler overnight? This could come dangerously close to parenting advice, but humor me on this one. You are in charge! Put the baby in a bouncy seat/swing/Bumbo seat/pack-n-play and get in the shower! Your baby will be fine and you won't stink.

I could even go as far as saying put on some earrings and a swipe of mascara and you'll really feel good about yourself. But maybe that's not really your thing. The point is, take care of yourself. If you like make-up and cute hair, keep at it. The more you take care of you, the better you will be at taking care of the little ones. It's not selfish or a waste of time. You need to feel like you. And if you like a pretty dress once in a while, exchange one for your spit up stained yoga pants and go for it. The better you feel, the better you will mother. This isn't just about your appearance, but it tends to be the first indicator of how well you are taking care of yourself.

We tend to put ourselves last when we become moms, and that shouldn't happen. Especially because the more it happens, the more commonplace it is. I remember shortly after having Olivia, I had changed her diaper in the backseat of my car because we were out and she, of course, had had a huge blow out. You know the kind, up the back and oozing out of pant legs. Real fun. After cleaning her up, we were strolling through the store, and I kept smelling poop. I couldn't get the smell away from me. On my drive home I must have wiped my nose or something, because I quickly realized the smell was coming from me. Upon further review, I noticed I had her poop under my nails! The grossest part of all was my "huh" reaction. Like this was no big deal and an expected part of life. Though I doubt any of you choose to keep your children's bodily fluids under your fingernails, the point is, when we become moms we tend to devalue ourselves. We don't get our hair cut, or we just throw it up in a messy bun; we don't buy that cute top, and just wear our worn out college t-shirts, and we succumb to thinking it's fine to have poop under our nails, so to speak. Value who you are—you deserve it!

Tip two: Get out of your house. This is good for you and your kids. It's easy when you stay at home to literally *stay at home*. But this can be, quite honestly, boring. Going out during the work week is your chance to get the good parking spaces and enjoy the short lines that weekends don't allow. Don't worry about the amount of stuff you (think you) need—load it up and explore. Go to parks, museums, or anywhere that piques your interest. And don't just go to kid-geared spots; take that baby to art exhibits, sit-down restaurants and Target. The more places you take your kids, the more they get accustomed to it and will behave accordingly. It will happen; trust me. Plus, you need fun in your life too. If the thought of an afternoon at a bouncy house place makes you see sideways, skip it and tell the kids you're going somewhere real exotic. You know, like Ikea.

Tip three: Get help. Asking for help may be hard for you. You may think that since you are at home all day you should have no problem getting everything done, or that since this is your "job" you shouldn't ask for help. This is false guilt talking. You will need help. That isn't a big deal! Whether you have a teen you trust who can play with your kiddos for a few hours, or a grandparent close by who'd love to spend time with them, use them. Even if it just means you get to go grocery shopping alone, if you have the help, use it. When I had three kids, four and under, the thought of taking all of them with me to any store whatsoever was terrifying, so a friend and I would trade time off with each other. She'd watch mine a few hours one day and I'd watch hers the next. It was great because it was free and the kids got to have time socializing. However help looks for you, do not feel guilty using it.

I did have good reason to feel guilty once, however, when I asked for help. We had a babysitter we used every so often who was a young teen. She was unavailable one night but she gave us the name of a friend of hers. We booked her and probably used her two or three times after. She was taller than me and definitely looked like an older teen. After chatting with her (and AFTER letting her watch my little ones), she mentioned something about being in fifth grade. She was only 10 or 11! I had just assumed that she was older but never even asked for sure. The icing on the cake was that she had given one of my kids some Tylenol without me ever giving her permission. I asked her how she knew how much to give and she snottily replied, "I can read, you know." Needless to say, we stopped using her! I readily admit I deserved that dose of mom guilt.

Though I didn't do a terrible job of asking for help, I certainly would have loved more of it. I can remember going through a particularly hard stretch. I was so tired, physically and emotionally, and in need of a good break, that I began to hope for a non-serious injury or sickness that would warrant me a night in the hospital. Just to get a night away! And a friend of mine once told me she often wondered what was the least bad thing she could do that would land her a night in jail. Who is so tired that a night in jail sounds like a day at the spa? Please don't let yourself get to that point. And especially don't rob a bank or something to get out of diaper duty!

Tip four: Keep doing what you love. Just because you've become a mom does not mean you have to stop doing the things that bring you joy outside of motherhood. Is it selfish? Nope. Is it fair to the kids? Yes! You will be a better mom when you go get your nails done or jog a few miles. Maybe you're crafty and just want to get away and craft your heart out. When my kids were little I loved to scrapbook. It's funny because when I needed a break from them, I'd go and make scrapbooks all about them. Seems counterintuitive, but it was what I found fun and it stimulated the creative juices that motherhood didn't. Plus it's a huge help now when I don't remember the stories and funny memories I was sure I'd never forget. They are all well-documented. (Spoiler—you do forget! Go buy a scrapbook.)

* * *

It's OK to admit if you're struggling.

I've tried to be as honest as I can about my time as a stay-at-home mom. I want you to be too. For me, I think I had romanticized the idea of it for so long that I had a very unrealistic expectation of how things were going to be. It took me awhile to realize that, but when I did I found some freedom in it. I came to see that my issues weren't revolving around new motherhood, though that was hard at times and an adjustment for sure, but it was uniquely tied to me staying home.

Please hear this, if you felt this way and chose to go back to work, there is nothing but respect from me. Staying home isn't for everyone. I just chose to push through because that is the path Mike and I had chosen for our family. I also had not gotten established in a profession I loved, so that definitely played a role. I wasn't missing a specific job, just the *idea* of one.

If you are struggling with staying at home, or anything else for that matter, please talk with someone. You need to decide whether you are going to stick it out (with changes made for your happiness!) or go back to work. You may just need a time frame that gives you an outlook into how long you will be committing—that alone can help. Deciphering whether your feelings are coming from postpartum depression is also a necessary step to take. You need to know if your struggles are related to staying at home specifically or could be more.

Above all, admit your struggle. If staying at home is not what you hoped it to be, powering through and not admitting it will not make you thrive. Whether you change your plan or not, if you want to enjoy where you are today, acknowledge what you are feeling. There is no shame; trust me!

* * *

Get Involved

My last piece of advice for you stay-at-home readers (and really all moms will benefit from this) is to get involved with a cause. Find your passion and be devoted to something bigger than you. Something bigger than your kids. Because, believe it or not, you will be a better mother if you have other areas you are pouring yourself into.

You have to pick something that is meaningful to you. You don't need to care about every cause, or be a part of every fundraiser that comes your way, but do pick what you believe in and pursue it. Get outside of yourself. This can look like a lot of different things. Whether you choose to grow spiritually and join a Bible study, want to give back by volunteering in a food pantry, or feel called to mentor other woman and start a moms' group, it doesn't matter. See a bigger picture than what is just inside the walls of your home—not doing so can be a dangerous by-product of staying at home. Plus, as a stay-at-home mom, you will never have the amount of unstructured time as you do right now, so why not put it to good use?

This is a two-fold win. It does good in the world—awesome! The world needs it. But it does good in you too. You will feel newfound fulfillment and have a bigger worldview. This is especially important for stay-at-home moms, I believe. Because as cliché as it sounds, the more you learn and grow as a woman, the more you will excel at being a mother.

"I know this is controversial, but I would say try to get your baby on a sleep schedule. Don't be legalistic about it, but routine helps everyone."

"I would say to get out. Don't stay in because you are worried about how your baby will behave. You need community and other moms around you, particularly moms in the stage ahead of you."

Kate from Illinois

Trust your mommy instincts. Sometimes a voice inside says I don't feel comfortable with this as a parent, or this isn't good for my kid. You may not have a valid reason you can articulate or even know the source of your concern, but TRUST IT.

Heather from Indiana

"Mommy will think about it."

Narrator: Mommy never did think about it. She knew it was a "No" all along.

IG:@loudmomma

CHAPTER FOUR

WORKING MOMS

I've only ever been a part-time working mom and it was after my kids were older and more independent, so I won't pretend for a second to know exactly what you as a working mom are going through. Your needs are unique to your situation. Some of you do traditional day care; some of you have family childcare. No matter your individual choice, you have unique mothering issues.

Can I let you in on a little secret? My stay-at-home mom friends may not like for me saying this, but…I think you guys just may have it harder. Not that I am making it a competition at all, because I hate that moms get that thrown at them. But it feels pretty true. You have many of the responsibilities of a stay-at-home mom alongside your full-time job. Finding the time for getting the house clean, shopping for groceries, or accomplishing most errands are tasks that are trickier to manage. I don't know how you do it! I started working part-time 12 years after being a stay-at- home mom, and just that amount of time threw me. All of a sudden things I had taken for granted became huge obstacles. How do I schedule appointments now? How will I get dinner ready at a reasonable time? When in the world will I get my roots done? Questions like this helped me realize just how much more working moms have to balance. So maybe instead of saying you have it harder, I will say you have a whole different set of circumstances than stay-at-home moms do, and that can absolutely play a significant role in the joy you feel while mothering.

So, I applaud you. I've observed enough of my full-time working mom friends to see with my own eyes the extra stress they are under and gain a new appreciation for the role they've chosen. One thing that I have observed from listening to many working moms is that mom guilt is one of their biggest issues. They either feel guilty about all the time away from their kids, or they feel guilty that they don't feel guilty. Pretty opposite ways of thinking. Working moms should not have to justify their choice. I hate the weight of mom guilt for any reason and working moms seem to deal with this the most. One of your biggest hurdles to overcome will be to free yourself from guilt.

So let's dive right in to how to do just that! My advice is interestingly enough the same I gave to stay-at-home moms...

* * *

Get Help

Remember when I said you can't have it all? You can't do it all either. Nor should you feel the pressure to.

Allowing yourself to receive help is paramount if you want to enjoy your motherhood. I am all for grocery delivery, car pools and cleaning services. Your time is precious, so don't feel guilty about using help. If your budget can support it, use the help and invest that time you save into your husband and kids. It will not be wasted. If you know your groceries will be appearing magically from Shipt or Amazon, and you know someone else dusted the baseboards (please, you'd never do that anyway, right?), then you are more freed up to enjoy your kids instead of feeling rushed, stressed and just barely surviving.

Are you afraid of asking for help? Do you worry that it makes you look weak or incompetent? Don't let that take root in your mind for a second, because for one, it's not true. And two, parenting is a long haul. You've got years and years of this ahead of you. If you are not allowing others to help, you will burn out fast. Your kids don't deserve that. You don't deserve that either. Call a grandma over and let her play while you run errands or scrub the shower (or pretend to scrub the shower but really take a nap—I won't tell). And, if you are married, you have a partner in this. Use your husband's help. Receiving help is absolutely not an indictment of your parenting skills, but it is a great way to thrive in motherhood.

Working part-time is forcing me to receive help more than I am used to. But what I am finding is that it's doing more than just providing help with getting kids where they need to be, or something else practical in nature. It's forcing me to admit that I can't do it all, and that is humbling. You may be very used to being productive at work—maybe you are even the boss. You are used to setting the tone for your employees and meeting deadlines. And then you come home from work and can't seem to throw dinner together. Or remember that kid number one has soccer practice at the same time as kid number two's dance recital, so how's that all going to work? Somehow the competence you feel at work falls to the wayside at home and you hear whispers of "you are failing at motherhood." You absolutely are not. You just need help. And maybe you need humbled too, so ask for help and don't let the seeds of feeling incompetent take root.

Two or three times this very month I have relied on my own kids to help me. That is another level of humbling because they are the very people I am trying to be capable for! But I realized that asking Riley to pick up a few things at the grocery store not only helps me, but it's good for him too. He likes feeling that I've relied on him. And I doubt he's ever thought I was falling apart because I forgot to pick up milk. When I asked Olivia to provide a ride for Madelyn to Driver's Ed, I let her see that it's OK to ask for help. If I pretend to always have it together in front of my kids, they won't feel the freedom to reach out for help when they need it too. So I am getting some assistance when I need it and providing them with some subtle life lessons—mothering win!

* * *

Own It

My next advice is some that I also gave moms who stay at home. If you've made your choice to be a full-time working mom, own it. Relax into it and let yourself excel at your job. There isn't a dad I know that doesn't think he can excel at work and be a dad at the same time. So why should moms? It's challenging of course, but absolutely doable. I have heard so many working moms say that they "have to work." It seems as though they feel the need to put that out there as a justification, lest anyone judge their full-time working choice. As if financial reasons are the only "right" reasons a mom can decide to work full-time. So not fair. If you love your profession and can't imagine not doing it, or you know you would not excel at staying at home, it's OK. Do not give into feelings of guilt regarding working full-time. As long as you are giving your children the love and attention they need from you when you are with them, they will grow up feeling secure in it. Remember, mom guilt is the biggest threat to enjoying motherhood. Don't let it fester and remember that you are the only one who has control over it.

A mom I know and love is Kate. She is a Pediatric Nurse Practitioner and works in a busy medical practice. She recounted a time that was especially hard on her as a working mom that I found heartbreaking. She had recently had her second child and he was struggling with sleep. She herself then was so sleep-deprived and felt she was not excelling at work, but also not at home. It all came to a head one day at work when she had a patient come in for a well-check and Kate was talking with the child's mother. The mom wanted tips about sleep training because her baby was still waking up once a night. Kate remembers feeling, in her words, like an "imposter" and even a "hypocrite." Here she was giving advice to this mom when her own child had been up about ten times the night before, and nothing she did would soothe him. I truly felt for Kate as she told me that story, understanding the stress she was under. She has since moved past these feelings, absolutely "owning" and excelling in her professional life. Her words were that in the beginning of motherhood you have to "accept that you will feel mediocre at all the things." Funny enough though, I have watched her over the years and have never once felt mediocre described her at all!

* * *

I think it's important to realize, especially for you as a working mom, that "mom" is not a job—it's a role. Whatever you do that provides income is your job. Being a mom is your role in the family—same as with stay-at- home moms. Your role as mom is as valuable and significant as a mom who stays home. Do not get caught up feeling less—than or insignificant in that role. Your husband's role as father does not hinge on whether he works 40 hours a week or not. He's dad and he's important. Same with you; your role is indispensable and not determined by workload. Let yourself truly believe that and feel some freedom from any unhealthy thoughts regarding your importance.

Scale Back

This probably seems so obvious that it's silly to write. But it seems to be one of the hardest things for parents to do. If you want to excel as a working mom, some things are going to have to take a back seat. This will look different for everyone. A school teacher will have more on her plate during the school year. An accountant's life will be crazy during tax season. So, certain seasons of life will be different, and you will have to be at peace with that. If work is super busy for a period of time, keep in mind that it won't last forever and don't allow it to be another link to guilt. This will be true of your husband's job as well, so the two of you stepping in and picking up the slack at different times will have to become commonplace.

Your kid's lives will have busier seasons as they get older too. Any parent with a kid in sports can attest to this. I was so excited when my kids tried sports the first time, but it was a strange change of pace to have my schedule revolve around theirs. Similarly, starting school changes things because all of a sudden your kids have their own calendar. It's a weird feeling when you have to juggle more commitments into your family schedule, especially when it's for little ones. And don't get me started on the month of December! Why does every school, group, and organization think December is the best month for a concert, program or banquet? Hit me up in January, please. Let's make it easier for everyone.

It's crucial during the busy stages to scale back in other areas. There is nothing wrong with politely declining invitations and any "extras" that come up. Having kids is the best excuse ever to get out of something, so use that to your advantage when necessary. Needing to spend time with your family is a completely valid reason to say no to others. You do not owe anyone anything that will compromise your happiness as a mom and wife, or your family's overall health. This is especially true for you as a working mom. Even if this means your kids decline a playdate or party invitation, your time is precious and cannot be dictated by what other people want you to do.

* * *

Lower Your Standards

Hmm, this probably sounds like terrible advice. But hear me out. If you are a working mom, you will not have the amount of hours in the day to do all the things you *think* you need to. You may think your baby will likely flunk out of high school if you don't take her to a Mommy and Me class. She won't. You may think your family will develop a horrible disease if you don't serve a homemade meal every night. They won't. You may think your mother-in-law will judge you for getting a cleaning service...she might. But who cares, this is about your joy in motherhood, not hers.

Truthfully, I think all moms should lower their standards at some point. I am writing this right now while we are quarantined from the Coronavirus pandemic and no other time in history has this truth been more evident. All over social media I am seeing mom after mom struggling. The immense stress on everyone is palpable, and I understand that. However, I also see moms trying so hard to (at least portray to) manage being stuck at home, helping kids with schoolwork and attempting to keep life somewhat normal. Then there are the ones that seem to be making it into a competition of who can be most creative, most fun, or most "on top" of things. I see the ones that are barely hanging on and I want to scream from the rooftops—you are doing just fine! Lower your expectations on what being the perfect mom is right now (and truly everyday)! Adjust your idea of what life should look like! Even when life is normal again I want us to believe those things. You can't thrive as a mother if you are constantly feeling like you aren't meeting some standard that you most likely are putting on yourself.

Your house, your yard, your body—whatever is causing you stress—is nothing compared to enjoying the time you have with the family you created. My sister Misty has realized she kept her standards too high when her kids were little. She says she never let herself stop to just have fun; she was always driven to "do." What a difference her day-to-day joy could have been if she hadn't done that. My friend Kristen says that she wishes she had stopped stressing about her house looking perfect. She feels she hampered hospitality and social situations by not thinking her home was up to some imaginary standard. She regrets not cultivating relationships with neighbors because of those fears. My other friend Jill had a different angle. When I asked her what lowering standards would look like for a mom of young kids, she mentioned shopping. That might look like buying Target jeans instead of a much more expensive brand, or buying groceries at Wal-Mart instead of Whole Foods, and thus ignoring that ridiculous notion that you aren't providing the best of the best.

So, whatever it looks like for you, be sure to put some safeguards in place. Make changes or instill some new mind-sets to stop putting unrealistic standards on yourself and your family. It may sound counter-intuitive, but it very well may be that the best way to "get the poop out of your nails" (and thus value yourself) is by lowering your standards. If they are too high and unattainable for your stage of life you could be setting yourself for failure without needing to. Lowering the standards you, or anyone else for that matter, has placed on you is a way to value your time, your sanity and your joy.

* * *

Lastly, I know that after working a full day or week, you feel you should make the time up and spend it all on your kids, because, mom guilt, right? By all means, spend the time. But I caution you to not neglect your husband. He needs you too. Just as much as you need quality family time, you also need quality alone time with him. One of the best ways to be a great parent is to invest in your marriage. Set up a monthly (or even weekly, if you can swing it) non-negotiable date night—something you can both look forward to and know is coming. Keep it sacred. Protect it. Of course, life happens and you may have to adjust at times, but do all you can to make it happen regularly. Hire a babysitter to watch those kids and have fun together! Remind each other why you got together in the first place. If finances are an issue, then farm the kids out and the two of you can enjoy being home alone together. There's something to be said for being home alone in your house without the kids. It feels somewhat scandalous, like when you were a teenager and didn't know when a parent would walk in. Use that to your advantage.

"I've been both a working mom and a stay at home mom. In both scenarios I say to pay attention/be observant of your child/children. Watch for good and bad changes in their behavior. Notice and encourage their gifts and talents. Sometimes things have to change for the betterment of the family."

Rory from Ohio

I see all these moms who can do everything, and I think…I should have them do some stuff for me.

TODAY Parents

"Don't spend all your time off with your kids. As a working mom you need to be able to recharge yourself so you can support your kids and be a supportive spouse. I spent a lot of time going from work straight

to wife or mom mode without breathing in between. It wasn't good for anyone."

Jenny from Ohio

"As a working mom I have to let things go and forgive myself more. I'm not as organized, my house isn't as clean and I'm tired more. So I keep my to—do lists shorter so I can feel good about what I do accomplish instead of guilty about what I don't."

Gail from Ohio

CHAPTER FIVE

MARRIAGE

I've touched on the topic of marriage a bit already, but let's dive a little deeper into it here.

First though, I want to address single moms. I want you to hear this loud and clear. You are undertaking a momentous task. Motherhood is the hardest and most worthy calling women will ever receive. So, doing it without the full-time support of a spouse deserves a ton of recognition. This chapter may not apply to you now—maybe it used to, or maybe it will in the future. So, skip it if you want. Read it if you want. Either way, I want you to feel supported and important, because you are. Being married is not at all an indicator of how good of a mom you are. Nor is it an indicator of how good of a woman you are. So, no guilt, right?

If you've been married for more than a few days, you know marriage is hard. Throw in a few babies, a few thousand diapers, a mortgage and pre-teen hormones (oh yeah, that's coming new moms!) and it can be a recipe for disaster. But it doesn't have to be. I personally hate the idea that marriage is the end—the end of fun, the end of freedom. It can be just the beginning!

* * *

Here's my most frank talk about your husband:

Your kids will grow up and leave your house...and you will only have each other.

This thought may depress you or it may send you into a happy dance. Either way, the truth is still there. You will only have each other at the end of this. So if you pour yourself into the kids without giving any of yourself to him, you will do damage. For one, you won't enjoy the child-raising years as much. It can be a tough time period, but you should do everything in your power to enjoy them. One way to accomplish this is by investing in the partner sharing all of these ups and downs with you.

Secondly, not only will you enjoy the child-raising years less, you'll enjoy the years after that less too. And those years are going to last a lot longer. If you are a newer mom, you may think the teenage/college years are far away. They are not. They will come faster than you think and will hit you like a ton of bricks. You will do yourself a favor to cultivate your relationship with your husband now so when the kids are gone you do not find yourself living with a stranger. Or a man you only tolerate.

I have heard from multiple women who truly fear their kids leaving the nest. Now, few moms are all-out excited about it, but I think some of the moms who fear it do so because they aren't looking forward to being alone at home with just their husband. Not wanting your kids to move out is one thing; not wanting them to move out because your marriage isn't strong is something else entirely. I had an older mom friend say she wished she had had more kids so that the empty nest years would be farther away. My thought was, what about when that eventual last kid did leave, though? You can't keep having kids just to ensure you aren't left alone with your husband. Maybe instead of being a mom of 20, take the time to develop your relationship with the man you have partnered with in the first place.

Mike and I have had a taste of this recently. With one kid in college, and our other two very involved with high school marching band, we have had a lot more time alone. Although it definitely feels a little weird, it's been a lot of fun too. We are bound and determined to enjoy our empty nest years and I think one of the reasons we will is all the work we've put into our marriage up to this point. The idea of my kids leaving home is less depressing when I focus on enjoying time with Mike. He and I can start a new chapter together that will still involve the kids; it'll just look different day to day. And it'll hopefully give us lots of grandbabies to spoil!

* * *

So, first things first. I love practical, doable advice, because sometimes you just need a set of marching orders.

Let him parent too.

Remember how you can't do it all? Let your husband share the load and you will never feel that struggle. I have seen so many moms complain that their husbands don't help. I get that. But my question is do you let him? Do you think he's capable? Does he know you want him to help? If you don't, and he doesn't, he won't.

If you want him to step up, tell him. Let me rephrase that—ask him. Share your frustrations and let him in on what you need from him. We live in a time where so many more dads are hands-on. I love that! I wouldn't survive as a mom if my husband wasn't that way, especially in the early years. So, don't stifle that in your husband. Encourage him and compliment him. It doesn't matter if he doesn't diaper as efficiently as you, or has a different parenting style altogether, let him know how much you appreciate his role as dad. If you belittle him or his fathering, you will destroy him. Do not expect him to get it right all the time, or do everything the same way you do. Remember, this is a journey for him as well. Make sure he knows he's just as valuable as you are. Because he is—you know that, right?

You will do yourself a huge favor if you dissect that one a little. Do you think your husband's role as a father is as important as yours as a mother? If you have to think about it at all, you probably don't. Examine yourself to make sure you are not undermining his role. All you have to do is talk with someone who grew up without their dad to see how indispensable the role is. Your roles will look different, especially if you are a stay-at-home mom, but both roles are equal in value. Remember that when you want to take over and do things "your way." His way may not be as good as yours, but it ultimately won't matter, barring a safety issue. His way just might be the best way, or it could at least create a unique bond with the kids.

I learned this early on. Soon after Olivia was born she started having a daily fussy time. Nothing I could do would soothe her—we all know how frustrating that can be. Well, Mike figured out a way to hold her that seemed to do the trick. He would lay her on her tummy on his forearm facing up, with her tiny head in his hand, and just walk around the house bouncing her. I was horrified the first time I saw this; thinking for one, it wasn't safe, and two, that it just looked plain weird. But sure enough, it did the trick and Olivia would always calm down and drift to sleep. I was smart enough, or maybe just that sleep-deprived, to simply be glad he found something that worked, instead of caring that I hadn't discovered it myself.

* * *

There's another aspect to my advice of letting your husband parent that you may not have considered: Working moms, do not think that since you are at work all day it's all on you in the evenings. If you put that extra stress on yourself you will be parenting out of desperation, not joy. Stay-at-home moms, do not think that because you stay at home you are always the one on call, including evenings. I always felt that once my husband got home from work we were a tag team. I had worked all day too. There is no reason for either parent to have to handle all the evening activities and chores alone. This will become more vital when your kids get involved in activities. For us, after dinner Mike would entertain the kids while I cleaned up. This was my call. Yes, he could and would have cleaned up, but I wanted him to have fun time with the kids, and I really wanted to load the dishwasher without someone attached to my hip. So it was a win/win. My point is, no matter your family's dynamic, expect your husband to be an active partner with you.

Maybe you're thinking you wish you had that problem. Maybe your husband is not hands-on and it's wearing on you and causing friction in your marriage. The only advice I can give you is to communicate. Fatherhood may not come naturally to him. He may feel inferior to you. Or he may just have his work/home priorities out of whack. You need to address it now. The early years are the hardest as far as needing physical help, so make sure he knows what you need from him. Like I said earlier, if he doesn't know what you need, he can't give it to you. If you think of this as a marital issue, not just a parenting one, it will hopefully spur you on to handling this problem. If you let it go, it will only become a bigger problem as you grow your family and the kids get older. If it continues to be a problem, as with any marital problem, seeing a counselor together can be a great step in getting back on track. Otherwise, bitterness sets in and your marriage will suffer for it.

* * *

My second word of advice for marriage support is:

Be united.

I can't pretend this is easy, but it is vital. Being a united front isn't just about good parenting, it's good for your marriage. Those little creatures have a way about them—they know how to divide and conquer! Your marriage is too important to let them do this to you and your husband.

Always strive to be united in front of your kids. This isn't just for older kids when things like curfew and dating comes up, but even with the baby/toddler stage. Most likely, one of you will naturally be the authoritarian and one will be more laid back and accommodating. This is actually a good thing, because you balance each other out. However, say you have decided to try sleep-training and plan to let your baby cry it out at bedtime. If one of you always goes in to rescue before the time you've agreed on, you're not united. If you've decided to take the pacifier away but one of you always caves and gives it to the child—not united.

As your kids get older, they get wiser, scarily fast. They will see this and they will take advantage of it! They need to see a united front. They need to see that mom has dad's back and dad has mom's. What a valuable way to model what a good marriage and partnership looks like to them. Plus, and trust me on this, they will know exactly which one of you to go to when they want something. It may be something simple now like a pacifier, but the teenage years are coming, and bringing a lot more complex issues with it. More than once my kids have come to me about something their dad already laid down the law on because they know which one of us is the softy!

The united front is not just for the kids' benefit. It's for the benefit of your marriage too. If you as a mom are constantly usurping dad, two things will happen. One, you will create a combative and unhappy atmosphere. No one wants to live that way. And two, he will step back. He will feel unnecessary and unimportant. If he does this to you, you will feel the same way and it becomes a vicious cycle. So fight the urge. Not all battles are worth fighting anyway.

Mike and I have had this issue pop up a number of times. He is the more authoritative one and I am— well he would say a pushover—but I like to call it being more agreeable. There are times when I disagree with him on something about the kids, but I try to talk to him about it privately. The times I have not done it privately always made the issue escalate and we ended up arguing in front of the kids. And sometimes I have to realize that he was right. Gulp. That can be hard, but if I value him as a dad, then accepting his input is para- mount. He decided a few years ago that the kids were taking over the mowing of the yard. We've had them doing chores since they were little, but nothing on a continuous or regu- lar basis. So, the kids weren't super thrilled with Dad's new idea. They moaned and groaned, and still now probably five years in, they still moan and groan about it. My inclination would be to let them get out of it or hire someone to do it. But Mike was adamant that they should do it, knowing the character-building it would bring, along with our belief that the whole family should pitch in with things. I actually do completely agree with him, so I stayed united with him on it instead of letting the kids whine themselves out of it. Better to keep my marriage happy anyway. And geez, it's not a big yard!

Mike has had to bend to me on a number of occasions as well. When our kids started school and began having homework, we had some different opinions on how this should look. In his home growing up, homework was done immediately after getting home, before any fun activities. I didn't have that experience and felt like kids need to blow off steam after being at school all day. I wanted the time after dinner to be "homework time," allowing the kids to have fun after school, and Mike to be home to help me—something that proved to be imperative when the kids got older and I could no longer help with math! He agreed with my plan and it's something we are still doing now. I appreciated him doing that for me, especially since he was the one to brush up on his algebra skills!

So, I hope you can see why the "united front" is included in the marriage chapter. It is a bigger issue than just being on board with each other, and does come dangerously close to my non-parenting advice promise. But if maintaining a solid marriage is as important to you as solid parenting is, you will heed this advice. You both need to feel supported and backed. Your flourishing as a mom, and his as a dad, depends on it.

Sex

You knew it was coming, right?! We can't talk about having a healthy marriage without discussing sex. Well, we could, but we'd be missing out! So, my sex advice?

Do it.

Did you just groan? Does it seem like just one more thing to you have to do?

New moms, I remember. The early years of babies and toddlers are not a sexy time. It's a wonder any of us conceive a second time. Between leaky breasts, the postpartum pouch and overall sleep deprivation, sex is usually the last thing you want to do. It's just hard to find the motivation. This time period is tricky. I will absolutely not tell you to "just do it."

My first experience struggling with feeling unsexy and uninterested in sex as a mom came before I even had my first baby. I was eight or nine months pregnant. Like I mentioned before, my whole body was pregnant. My stomach started right under my breasts and I couldn't even see where it ended. So, I was feeling very self-conscious about it and wouldn't let Mike see me naked. He was very encouraging and reassured me that he still found me attractive and there was no reason to feel insecure. One night I was undressing and decided he was right, I shouldn't hide myself. I took off my shirt and was only wearing my bra and super sexy maternity jeans. You know the kind, right? They have that huge panel that goes over your entire baby bump? I was standing there exposed, in all my pregnant glory and Mike looked up at me and said, "You look like the back end of a horse!" I stood there, blinked a few times and immediately burst into tears. What? Did he just call me a horse's ass? This was his idea! Realizing what he just said—and he's kind of notorious for sticking his foot in his mouth—he quickly explained himself. He said my jeans and bra reminded him of one of those animal costumes that two people wear together and I looked like the person in the back with suspenders. Oh man. His explanation only helped a little at the moment, but now, 20 years later, we laugh about this story all the time.

There is so much going on emotionally and hormonally when you're a new mom. So, maybe instead of saying "do it," I will say, "do it some." Sexual intimacy is a very important aspect in a marriage—it's actually vital if you want to keep your marriage healthy. I know what you're thinking...sex is what started this whole mess to begin with, right? Just please know this stage doesn't last forever. Believe it or not, you will want to do it again at some point. But don't put him off every time. I so don't want to sound like a 1950's housewife—never view sex as a duty or something you have no control over—but you should try to do it periodically. Because if you are still in that new mom haze where just getting through the day seems monumental, sex is probably not high on your to-do list. But the longer that is the case, the longer it will become your norm. You may need to remind yourself of the advantages of having sex on a regular basis. It may not be on your mind, but I am pretty confident it is on your husband's! Mike and I have found the more regularly we do it, the more in sync we are with each other in every other way. It seems he needs it more physically and I need it more emotionally. Both are valid reasons and both of us deserve to have our needs met. If nothing else, try and regard sex as an act of love for your husband. Talk to him about it, though. Let him know it isn't him per se, but just overall new mom-ness. My hope for you is that he is understanding and encouraging. If after several months you are still struggling to desire sex, it may be a good indicator of a bigger issue. Find someone with whom you can talk about it.

One Mother's Day early on in being parents, Mike said to me, "Well, since its Mother's Day, we DON'T have to have sex." What a gift, right? It was funny, and he was *mostly* joking when he said it, but I did struggle for a while with desire versus duty. Sometimes I had the mindset of "let's just do it and get it over with" and other times I felt like if I had one more person trying to touch me, slobber on me or even look at me, I might explode. But those feelings and that stage didn't last, thankfully! You will come out of that baby mom funk at some point and actually feel sexual again.

You also have to understand the inherent difference between men and women. Typically, men can just think about sex and they are ready to go. You, probably not so much. This is important to talk to your husband about. He may need to be reminded that you still like to be wooed a bit. One time when our kids were elementary age, I was standing at the sink doing dishes and Mike said something sexually suggestive to me. I pretty much ignored it and he got miffed. So I said, "You know what is actually sexy to me?" He absolutely did not. I said, "You playing with our children is sexy. You giving me a break and taking them outside is sexy. Hearing your sexy talk is not." (Or at least what *he* thought was sexy talk.) Without saying a word, he turned on his heels, gathered up the kids and took them to play on the swing set in our backyard, which I could see from the kitchen window. I cracked up, because boy, he played it up good that day. Swinging the kids, helping them down the slide and running all around, making sure I could see him. It may have been for selfish reasons, but he really did make me happy in that moment. We both would have missed out if I hadn't told him what I was feeling.

Older moms, guess what? Sex can get really good at this point. Your kids are getting more independent, but they are still innocent to what mom and dad are really doing when they say they are "napping" (or "wrestling" if you get caught!). Enjoy this stage. Use it to your advantage. I remember a friend of mine telling me that the month of December was the best month for sex because she would tell her kids that mom and dad were going to wrap Christmas presents and the kids would happily leave them alone. Whatever works, right?

Once your kids are even older, pre-teen and teen years, sex can be trickier, because they are way more aware of things than they were before. But they probably recoil at the thought of their parents having sex and are confident you are not doing it! Mike goes to bed pretty early to get up early for work, so summertime is tricky for us because we don't go to sleep at the same time—I generally like to stay up later with the kids. So, one night I told my daughter I was going to go up and say goodnight to Dad. I came back 30 minutes or so later and she gave me a long hard stare and said, "You were up there for a really long time…" Maybe she was on to me?

On the flip side, sex can get better at this stage in that teenagers are busy people and are gone a lot. This can translate into fun for your marriage. Watching your kids grow up can be hard, but having more fun time together as a couple can make up for it. Determine now that you will enjoy the time together and do the things you couldn't before.

* * *

One Last Thing

One last tidbit I want to share regarding marriage revolves around a popular saying. "Never go to bed angry" is something you have most likely heard before. You probably got this advice at your bridal shower. Someone, or several someone's, wrote it to you in a pretty journal filled with good intentions. But what Mike and I have come to see is that sometimes going to bed angry is the best thing you can do. Why? You wake up and realize that what made you mad the night before really isn't a big deal. Or you forget about it altogether. You wake up refreshed and notice that the annoying thing he said to you was just that—annoying. Not something to start a fight over. Obviously this won't apply to all issues, but we've come to notice the silly ones that happen in the evening when we are most tired and worn out are the ones that can, but don't need to, escalate the most.

"That first year with your first child is exceptionally hard and all you have is each other, which is good and bad. You have to rely on each other. This can further build your relationship as a couple. But what about when you as the mom are losing it (up all night, the kid isn't napping, STILL won't latch on, you have laundry and dirty dishes up to the ceiling, you haven't shaved your legs in ten days and it was only one leg, you haven't showered in four and you are eating cereal with water in it at 2:32 a.m. because you are out of milk) and the husband is working late or traveling?"

Heather, hilariously, from Indiana

"Be intentional in showing each other affection in front of the kids. They need to see a picture of a healthy relationship. They may groan and pretend to be super grossed out, but they actually really like seeing it. It gives them security and will give them a model to emulate in the future."

Me!

Sometimes I question my parenting, but to be honest, sometimes I question my child's childing.

Mommy Needs Vodka

CHAPTER SIX

PARENTING OLDER KIDS

This chapter will be the hardest one for me to write, but maybe the easiest, because this is the stage I'm currently in. Though I can't say I'm an expert, I am definitely in the trenches at the moment. Someone told me years ago that parenting babies and toddlers is physically exhausting and parenting teenagers is emotionally exhausting. This is proving to be very true.

When I had my kids, I didn't think the timing all the way through when it came to their ages. I really liked the idea of them being close in age; I liked the thought of doing the whole baby and toddler stage at once. But I didn't think about the fact that I would have three teenagers at once too. My favorite ages were from five to ten years old, and for me, that was the sweet spot of parenting. They are old enough to get up on a Saturday morning alone and they still really like you. They can play independently and they still say adorable things. Because the teen years follow so close behind, it can really take you by surprise to see how quickly they change. Now in general, I think teens get a bad rap—they can be really fun and witty. Mine are so goofy and surprise me in so many ways. I wouldn't trade this stage to go back to the toddler years; I'll take teen meltdowns over toddler ones any day. But at the same time, parenting teens is not for the faint of heart. Trust me on this one.

I do think the preteen and early teen years are the hardest emotionally. The ages of 11-14 are kind of freakishly awful. Your sweet baby turns into this hormonal, pimply, stinky, person who is bigger than you. (Mine were, at least—it was very strange to be asking my ten-year-old daughter to get me something off a high shelf!) But they're still pretty immature. They aren't sure who they are, you certainly don't know either, and it's all a matter of trudging through. Girls seem to have it the worst, but I believe the sooner they start their period, the better for everyone. The lead-up to the first one can feel like the longest battle of PMS ever, but after that, she (and thus, you!) gets a release of all that pent up angst. At least until the next month.

My dear Grandma-in-law, Mike's beloved grandma, said once, "Little kids, little problems. Big kids, big problems." This has definitely been the case in our home. Not to say there aren't major issues that come with little kids. Obviously health issues and such are huge battles to confront. But in general, the older your kids get, the harder it is to tackle the stuff that gets thrown at you. Dealing with a bully at age four is way different than at age 14. Finding your daughter kissing a boy at three is cute—at 13 not so much! And all of a sudden things like depression, suicide, STD's and drugs become an all-too-real area of parenting. As Mom, you have to find a way to rise to the challenge. Parenting teens is difficult on many levels—if you want to thrive, then you have to do due diligence.

* * *

Stay on Top of Things

There are so many things coming at teens. If you've used the internet much at all, you know the danger it poses to our kids. Add in social media and you've got all kinds of junk to deal with. You have to set rules and limits. My kids know that (while they are still teens) I follow them on social media and will stalk them at will. They are also aware that Mike and I believe strongly that their phones and laptops are fair game—we will look through their histories and text messages. Don't for a second think they like this or are cool with it. They are not, but we don't care. When I found out one of my kids had a "finsta" (a secret Instagram account for outsmarting parents), I hastily made them delete it. Later I was asked if they could restart it on the condition that I could follow it. This was their idea, which I thought was reasonable, so I agreed. You see, my job as their mom is to be aware of what is in their world that can harm them, whether it's physical or virtual. I have said plenty of times, it's not that I don't trust them, it's that I don't trust the world around them. Trusting your teen and staying oblivious to what they are doing is not the same thing. So many "good kids" easily get caught up in all sorts of temptations; it's no respecter of persons, especially teenagers!

Staying on top of things also gives you a great glimpse into their friendships and helps you know who is and isn't the best influence. I found this out firsthand when Olivia was in sixth grade and we were just getting into teen parenting. Text messages I read from her friends threw me for a loop—I had no idea these "sweet" girls she was hanging around used the foul language they did. I don't want to venture too far into parenting advice in this area (because I promised I wouldn't!) but I will say this: If you know what your teens are up to—what is truly going on in their world and what they are opening themselves up to—you will feel better as a mom. You will know that you are keeping tabs on the people you love the most because they matter the most to you and your heart is to protect them. In turn, your self-confidence as a mom will increase as you realize that you are doing what's hard and unpopular because of a bigger picture.

Limits can also be very clear cut and practical. There are many apps and tools out there to help. For example, we have set our Wi-Fi to turn off at certain times, limiting when the kids can, and more importantly, cannot, have internet access. It's very obvious when this time has come at our house. You will hear a collective sigh, and general gasp of disgust, from wherever a teenager is lurking.

We also use an app that has been so useful; I wish I could kiss whoever created it. It's called Life 360 and it is basically a tracking system. Now, before you think I am some weird stalker that doesn't trust my kids, think about whether your kids are driving yet. Or dating. Or "just hanging out with friends,

Mom." We got this app because not all of us have iPhones, so the Find my Friend app wasn't right for us. I can see where my kids are or at least where their phones are (and who are we kidding, no teenager is ever without their phone). It is a God-send once your kids are driving and you want to make sure they arrived somewhere safely, but don't want to call or text them in case they are still driving. Or if you have a kid who is going to a sleepover, you can make sure they are where they say they are. I use it for Mike too because historically I have *possibly, maybe* gotten paranoid if he's running late, and I am sure he's dead in a ditch somewhere. I can't tell you how many times I used to call him just to hear him answer and say, "I'm on our street!" (He knows me.) This way I can check, see that he is indeed on our street, and not have to call him. The kids use it too—Riley told me he likes to check in during school to see where we all are; I think it's cute that he's protective that way. But one time Olivia texted me and I hadn't gotten around to texting back. I quickly got another text from her saying, "I know you're at Target!" So, you know, it goes both ways. I can get called out too.

* * *

There is another way to thrive as a mom of older kids. It's not an easy one, but you have to...

Let them go.

One of the first, kind of preliminary ways you start letting go happens between the ages of 15 and 16. Somehow the state you live in thinks it's totally normal for your baby to get behind the wheel of a car and actually drive it? Boy, this is a hard one for me. The first time Olivia drove, Mike took her to a parking lot and let her just try it out. She said, "I love that sound!" Mike asked, "What sound?" Olivia happily answered, "The sound of acceleration!" Yikes.

I quickly learned that I hate, no abhor, teaching my kids to drive. I do admit that I tend to be a nervous passenger anyway, but being the passenger to my kid who barely remembers to brush their teeth, that's a whole new level of trust. It's awful, I'm awful, and the whole thing goes badly. I am normally a pretty calm person. I certainly lose my temper and have yelled at my kids plenty of times, but I'm definitely not a screamer—until I'm in the passenger side of the car with them. I am also not much of a swearer—it's just not something I like to hear, so I made a commitment at the beginning of motherhood to not cuss in front of my kids. Well, I have broken that commitment more than once now while riding with my teenage drivers! Thankfully Mike does not scare easily and he has taken over most of this task. It wasn't any better with Riley than it was with Olivia and I'm learning now with Madelyn that the third time is *not* the charm. But you do have to get used to it, no matter how strange it is when your kid gets their license and can legally drive away from your house on real roads to wherever they want! The first time Olivia drove off by herself I had tears streaming down my face. Letting go had a whole new level of meaning. If you haven't started praying for your child yet at this point, you will. And you'll go get that app.

Letting go then gets even harder. I know this firsthand because this is the season we're currently in. All three of my kids are at the point where they're launching into adulthood. When I began writing this book Olivia had just left for her first year of college. So I have had a lot of time to process this whole thing—this new chapter of life. I've come to realize something pretty important: I'm OK. Now, full disclosure, she is only 30 minutes away. If she were hours and hours away, I may be a blubbering mess as I write this. Her whole senior year of high school, I felt like I was grieving. Her leaving was like this looming end date. It felt like a roller coaster—it was super slow going up that first hill, but then it was going to whisk her away from us in a flash. The weeks between graduation and college move-in day felt like a whirlwind and I had to constantly tell myself "this is not going to break me." When the day came and Mike and I had to leave her, there were tears for sure (lots for me and none for her), but I was OK. I didn't think I would be able to leave my baby at this huge intimidating school. She goes to The Ohio State University, with over 64,000 others. But I did it and I learned something—I *can* let go, I had just taken a huge step. And it didn't have to wreck me or send me into a depression.

I decided to look at her going to college as the gift it was. For one, she scored herself a really good scholarship because she was a strong student in high school. And two, I thought about how many girls all over the world don't even get to finish high school, let alone attend a major university. Neither of those things made it easier to let her go, but how can I dismiss a blessing like that? I made myself just be happy for her and excited for her new experiences, instead of selfishly thinking how it was affecting me. What a relief that was. Like I mentioned before, the whole goal of parenting is to raise independent adults. I was literally watching this take place and I couldn't let my sadness overshadow it.

Until the following Tuesday. We have a tree in our front yard that somehow became "the tree." It's where we always take pictures on the first day of school and for special events like dances. So, that first year it was really hard when Riley and Madelyn had their first day of school and I was only taking their pictures and not Olivia's. That previous Saturday was when we had dropped her off and I had cried every single day after. Tuesday morning came and I thought, "I'm fine. I'm not going to cry today." Well, not even an hour later I got a text from Olivia. It was a picture of her with her book bag going to her first class at OSU. And she was standing in front of a tree. You can be sure I bawled at the sight of it. I adored the picture, but also her for knowing how special it would be for me to have it. And here I am now crying while writing about it!

What I've learned during all of this is that I can be happy for my kids growing up and feel sad about it at the same time. Both emotions are real and valid. I have to give myself the freedom to feel both things. It feels more like grieving the end of the age. We aren't all home for family dinners together anymore and they aren't all safe in their bedrooms, tucked in by Mike or me. And when Olivia, and soon the others, comes home, it's a visit. I hate that thought the most—that they are just visiting home and not *just home*. Maybe until they are truly living independently I won't look at it that way. But mother-hood never really ends, so if I am going to keep thriving, I have to learn this now, whether they are in my home or not. I have decades ahead of me—I don't want to spend them depressed because this stage is closing.

So, whether you are close to this stage or not, determine now that you will deal. The teenage years kind of make it easier because they can be rough. I know plenty of parents who were thrilled when they were empty nesters. But I don't think it matters whether your kids are super challenging or not—it's hard to let go. It's hard to not be there all the time and hard to not help them make good decisions. For me, because Olivia is extremely independent already, I wasn't too worried about her leaving. She had proven to be level-headed and responsible. But, I just like her and I like having her around. So, that has been the hardest part for me—getting used to a new normal.

* * *

Let them struggle.

Say what? Here's some tough love for you: Sometimes you have to use tough love with *them*. This doesn't start with the teen years, but the teen years are when you will see the need for this show up the most. It is in our very nature to protect our kids, shield them and make life easy. However, that isn't always what's best for them.

I recently read an article about Millennials. Sorry, I just may be talking about you here, but the premise of the article was that twenty-somethings are the most educated group in history, but many can't do simple things like cook a meal. A large amount can't balance a checkbook or do their laundry. I don't want my kids to be college educated, but unable to function as adults. So, even though it's for their benefit, I personally want to look back and see that I raised really awesome humans, and know I excelled as a mom by teaching them how to do certain things without just doing it for them. I will know that *I* excelled if I can watch *them* excel.

There are countless ways this can happen, but I will share a couple tangible ways we have tried to create this kind of learning environment in our family. For one, we've always had chores for the kids to get in on. We've stressed that we are all in this together and everyone pitches in. On a side note, I've been intentional that Riley also cleans the kitchen and bathrooms and does typical "girl chores." Mike's mom taught him to clean growing up and I completely appreciate it—he isn't a slob that expects me to pick up after him. So hopefully I get points with Riley's future wife. We also have made the kids get part-time jobs when they get their licenses to pay for their car insurance. I know a lot of teens are busy with sports and activities, but I think there is so much value to learning young about the value of money and how to budget. And nothing shakes entitlement out of a teenager like working fast food.

Letting them struggle can be more than just showing them how to make mac and cheese or working at McDonald's, but also about how to get through hard times. If our reaction is to always rescue them, they never learn how to push through anything.

Sometime around Olivia turning nine or ten, we were getting very concerned about her shyness. Not that shyness itself is bad, but it was beginning to cripple her. So Mike decided that she would start ordering for herself at restaurants, something she would never do, as a small step towards moving through it. Olivia was not happy at all and the first time she had to do it, she was in tears at the table and speaking so quietly the server couldn't even hear her. I sat there with tears myself because it was so hard for me to watch her struggle. I really wanted to jump in and save her but I knew this was the right thing. Each time she did it, it got easier, and within a few months it wasn't a problem for her anymore. She may very well have gotten through that on her own, but I'm glad it was while feeling safe with her family, rather than off on her own in college.

If you want them to thrive, let them struggle. Let them figure things out and you will create thriving adults. Don't unintentionally handicap them by doing everything for them. This is for your sanity too—you have enough on your plate as it is—let them handle their plates. And their school projects and Valentine's Day boxes and homework, for that matter. Don't let me find out you are doing fifth grade math again! I once took my kids on a playdate where the mother sat next to her son while he played video games. He wouldn't stop to eat so she sat right next to him and put food in his mouth for him, even going so far as telling him when to "open." She said it was too much of a fight to get him to stop playing, so she just spoon-fed her four-year-old bite after bite. I often wonder how that kid is faring now in college.

* * *

But also, listen to them talk.

I want to be clear, when I say "let them struggle," I absolutely don't mean leave them alone or don't be there for them. You can't thrive in motherhood if you aren't sure you know who your kid is. Or what your kid loves. Or what is going on in their world. The only way for you both to enjoy this relationship is for you to listen. The teen years are so formative. They are inundated with so much information all day, every day, and they need to be able to process it. Not all of them will, of course. But, I encourage you to try and keep on trying. Don't give up even if they are slamming doors in your face— they need to know you want to hear from them when they are ready.

In our family, this has not quite followed the stereotypes. For the most part, when I have asked my girls, "How was your day?" I get a "fine," "ugh," or possibly a "meh." When I ask Riley the same question, he will start with, "Well, in my first class..." Ten minutes goes by and he's just gotten to lunch. He loves to talk and is happy to oblige. My girls, not so much. But the older they get, the more they do start to open up, so take heart, pre-teen moms.

The key to listening to them is to actually listen and let them do the talking. Chances are they want to sort out life with you, but they want to know you are a good and trust-worthy listener. So put your phone down and give them your full attention. This is especially true when they are dealing with dating. They need you to listen. Believe me, I know this is hard. One of my girls was dating someone we weren't too excited about. He wasn't a bad person, just not the right fit for her. I found myself talking too much about it with her, which was shutting her down more than anything. So I laid off a bit (but you can believe I prayed hard instead!) and just let her talk and work through it. When the break-up did eventually happen, I was very glad I was still a confidant instead of being avoided because I hadn't been a good listener. A mostly good listener, anyway.

In full transparency, I had to relearn this lesson just the other day. Madelyn was going through something and I very clearly thought I had all the answers. As I tried to console her, it became evident quickly that I was actually just lecturing and was close to losing her in that moment. I basically told her I'd stop talking and just hold her while she cried if that is what she really needed. Guess what? It was. So, I held her, she cried, and all it took was being there for her and letting her get out what she needed to.

In my experience so far in parenting teens, I have come across a few tricks to get them talking. First, there is something about being in the car that brings out conversation. I don't know if it's because I'm not staring right at them, but I do find that they are slightly chattier while driving. Take advantage of that while they are young because once they start driving themselves everywhere, you lose a lot of alone time with them. While this may be sad to hear, I have to say, you may not hate losing your role as taxi driver, so it is definitely a trade-off. Try it out next time you are in the car; just be sure to use very open-ended questions. "Yes/no" questions never get you anywhere with a teenager. I have literally asked, "Can you tell me one specific detail about your day?" just to get something more than "It was fine."

Secondly, as much as I hate how technology has taken over their worlds, I definitely use it to my advantage. If I sense one of the kids is struggling with something, or is unusually quiet, I will send them a funny GIF, a Pin I think they'd like, or just text them saying I love them. It doesn't always open the floodgates, but I feel better knowing that I am doing something to show I care. The times they write back, or send me something funny back, I know they like communicating with me that way too. Sometimes with teens, you have to take what you can get. So if all you get is a silly meme, relish it. You can look forward to your older kids getting better at this. Recently I have gotten texts from Olivia asking me how my day was; this is kind of revolutionary, because if you haven't noticed, teens are a wee bit self-centered. Having one ask me about what's going on in my life gives me a dose of hope that my hard work of parenting may just be paying off.

Lastly, food. Teenagers love food. I have used this trick many times, and hopefully I am not creating emotional eaters who run for Dairy Queen at every problem, but getting them out for coffee or ice cream together can open up communication pretty remarkably. Riley and I have a coffee date quite often—I love that we have "our thing" and he loves it too. He also loves the fact that I pay. Mike has tried to regularly take each kid individually for donuts on the weekends. It's been his special one-on-one time with each of them that has proven to *sometimes* get them talking.

Just keep in mind that not all kids want to talk to their mom about certain stuff. You can't force them to talk; you most likely didn't share every detail with your own mom. Promise me you won't take it personally. Even if it stings a bit, try to find other people in your kids' life that they will talk to and just be glad they have someone, even if that someone isn't you. All three of my kids have become close to leaders in their youth group at one point or another and I am beyond grateful for that. They need other adults who pour into them and care for them.

* * *

Finally, to enjoy motherhood with older kids:

Have fun!

Having fun with teenagers? Is that a thing? I won't lie and say it is every day, but it does happen. The thing I've learned while parenting teens is that they are like little emotional roller coasters. You never know when a huge loop is coming and their mood will totally change. These swings can be good or bad—if they're in a junk mood, you get very relieved when that roller coaster rolls in and takes the angst with it. But, oh, when things are fine and you are going about your day and bam! Eye rolls, heavy sighing, door slamming, and any number of various "loving" remarks can be uttered. (Hopefully I am not describing you!) This is really rough when you have more than one teenager because you can never predict when that perfect moment is going to come around when they are all happy at once. When it does happen it can feel like a rare solar eclipse or something.

My best advice is to not let it bother you. I have not mastered this, let me be totally honest. But life is so much easier when I don't take these mood swings personally, or worse, join in on them. One time when one of my girls, who will remain nameless, was 13 or 14, we were all discussing where we were going to go out to dinner. Nothing sounded good to her, nor could she come up with any ideas. So we just made a decision and said that's where we were heading. I kid you not; my normally level-headed child slid to the floor, curled up into the fetal position and proceeded to cry "Nooooo!" I can't remember if tears were involved or not, but I think the chances are 99%. Mike and I just stood there staring at her like, "Who is this person?" It happens, and you, Mom, have to let it blow over. Fighting through it never works. Correct behavior when needed, but know that soon, or possibly in five to six days, she will be back to herself.

Under this "have fun" category is another component and it's so simple. Laugh. The best way to have fun with them and stay connected is to laugh together. Teenagers can be so funny, many times without even trying to be! One time I was giving Riley a lecture about working hard in school and

I said something along the lines of, "Teachers love seeing their students show effort." His response was, "Yeah, they dig binders too." He surely was listening to my important life lesson. So sometimes you might be laughing *at* them instead of *with* them.

Chances are your kids do not see you as a fun-loving, silly person. You are the one always on them to finish homework and clear the dishes. So it's good for you to let your hair down and be carefree with them once in a while. Watch TikTok's with them, find a show on Netflix to watch together or be really crazy and show up at school as a surprise and take them out to lunch. Because remember, food. Just allow yourself the freedom to have fun if you want to enjoy these teen years.

* * *

Another way to have fun with them is to...

Be interested in what they are interested in.

This seems pretty obvious, I know. Especially because as you've parented little kids, you probably have already grown an odd affection for a cartoon character that you never expected. Or you now love a TV show or movie in a way you didn't see coming. I still feel a fondness for The Wiggles, stemming from Riley's total obsession with them as a three-year-old. This can get easier when your kids get older because their interests mature, thankfully. You will do yourself a favor to dive into what those interests are because it gives you common ground. That is a hot commodity with teenagers, so if you still want to flourish as a mom of teens, do your homework.

A few years ago, Olivia was obsessed with the band One Direction. Full on teenage fandom. She had posters of them all over her room, plus all the merchandise you can think of. And you can imagine her complete, utter joy when they released a song titled "Olivia." So, I have to tell you I know more about that band than I would have ever wanted to. I listened as she talked and sighed over those guys. Of course, she grew out of her obsession, but now when I hear about any of the band members or see a picture, I get a little twinge of sadness because it reminds me of that time and how fun it was to watch her first crazy teen antics. I had no interest in them as a musical group, but I had every interest in staying engaged in my teen's life. Thankfully Madelyn has much better taste in music and I am currently hearing all about Twenty One Pilots and Panic! At the Disco.

This is where I have to tell on myself. Because, sigh…Riley is a huge Star Wars fan. Beyond just watching the movies, he loves watching YouTube videos all about the storylines and side stories and conspiracies. I "listen" to him talk about these things. But I have zero interest in any of it. I just can't quite care. So, no, you won't always love what they love. And sometimes listening to their world is more boring, than well, Star Wars is for me. But you have to focus on the fact that you love them and muddle through somehow!

Enjoying parenting teens comes down to this: It's not always fun. Neither were the toddler years though, right?

Each stage has its obstacles. Your job is to adjust to it. The teen years don't have to be difficult, and being intentional about enjoying them will make all the difference. And please know our family has had a fair share of rough teenage moments. I haven't mentioned many because I want to respect their privacy, but we have run the gamut with issues regarding depression, anxiety, and general terrible decision-making on their parts. There have been numerous times where I have felt defeated and completely ill-equipped for parenting, in a much scarier way than what newborn and toddler parenting bring. But I love those three kids fiercely, so I push through. I remind myself that the hard times from when they were little really don't matter anymore and are even funny. My hope is that ten years from now I feel the same way about these current hard times!

Going into a teenager's room is like taking a trip to Ikea... you pop in just to look and end up leaving with six cups, two plates, three bowls, a tea towel and some cutlery.

DumpaDay.com

Having a teenager is like having a cat that only comes out to eat and hisses if you try to pet it.

@saucynthesuburbs

Listen to your teens and don't overreact.

Take time each night to say goodnight in their rooms—they seem to open up most then.

Kristen in North Carolina

When we take the time to sit at the table and eat as a family (and it definitely doesn't happen every night) I feel like everyone talks more, shares more and usually we laugh a lot together.

Holly, from Ohio

CHAPTER SEVEN

HEALTH

This chapter might scare you more than the sex talk. You might be dreading it, confident I'm going to shame you into eating nothing but kale and enduring hours of exercise. Relax! If you've recently had a baby, all I want you to do is sleep. Sleeping can do more for your health than a burpee right now.

I was a Personal Trainer and Weight Management Specialist on the side for five years and I actually love to help people eat "clean," learn how to exercise and live overall better lives. But I also think it's about balance. It's not about obsessing or stressing. Getting skinny should not be your goal. Nor should looking like your pre-baby self. A small, genetically blessed percentage of moms will see their pre-baby size. Your goal should be to live the healthiest version of you. By all means, eat your greens and use a treadmill, but also cut yourself some slack.

Exercise

When you feel ready and have been cleared to exercise, try to give it a go. There is a ton of evidence out there proving how regular exercise lifts your mood and creates balance in your life—something I'm guessing you might be wanting right about now. If you exercised regularly before pregnancy, and especially if you kept up with it while pregnant, this will be easier for you. But your body is forever changed, and your sense of balance may be off. So ease in to it. The great thing about a newborn is they happily go where you go. Strap that baby into a stroller or a sling and get walking. Your baby will love it and will most likely sleep the whole time (if you are lucky) and you will love moving your body.

As your child ages, and most likely more children make their entrance, you will naturally have to adjust. My best advice as a personal trainer was that you don't need a gym to get a great workout. Walking and jogging are the easiest, cheapest exercises there are. You can literally do it anywhere. If that's not your thing, one of my favorite workouts I call "Five for Five." It's where you pick your five favorite exercises—make sure at least two are cardio moves—and perform each exercise five reps for five sets. So it could look like this: five sit-ups, five burpees, five push-ups, five jump squats, and five lunges. Repeat that four more times for a total of five sets. As you progress, do eight moves, eight reps, eight times. It's a great way to structure a workout at home when you aren't sure what to do but want to do something.

There are so many resources to take advantage of. Find a great YouTuber or pull out your old Jillian Michaels DVD's and go at it. Pinterest has an amazing assortment of great workouts that usually require very little space or equipment. But maybe you are a gym rat. You love going to classes and enjoy the social aspect of it. If that is you, then get yourself there! The great thing about gyms is there are so many with childcare available. It's truly an investment worth making. The main objective is to do what works for you and what you'll actually enjoy doing and stick with it.

I personally hate yoga. I've tried to like it but I just don't. You may love it—knock yourself out! Just do something. A lot of moms think it's selfish if they work on themselves. I know working moms can feel this way because they are already away for work and feel bad taking more time from the kids. All I can say to that is don't take yourself on that guilt trip. Your health matters too. You deserve to look and feel good, and that is not selfish. You'll also be setting a great example for your kids. They will learn good habits by watching you. If the mom guilt does creep in, find ways to exercise with them. Family hikes and bike rides are great ways to incorporate exercise with family time.

I got pregnant the second time so soon after having my first baby, I didn't lose a lot of weight in between. I was bound and determined to get it off faster after having Riley, but I have to admit it was slow going. Or actually, I was slow going. I had a wedding to be in and had used my "I'll for sure be this size by the time of the wedding" reasoning for my bridesmaid dress. A month before the wedding I tried it on, and nope, I definitely was not that size. So I crash dieted—not something I ever advise—and did fit into the dress by the wedding. But guess what? One month later I got pregnant with Madelyn and it was years before I saw that size again!

At some point we have to accept that our bodies change during pregnancy and childbirth. But you don't have to pretend to love the changes. I am happy that I got to carry three wonderful humans and bring them into the world, but I can't pretend to enjoy the havoc they left in the process! I can't jump on a trampoline without peeing my pants. And I am covered in stretch marks. I don't love them, but I do love how I got them. After breastfeeding my last baby I noticed my bras just weren't fitting right. I decided to suck it up (no pun intended) and get professionally fitted for a new one. The sweet older woman who was working with me finally said, "what cup size have you always worn?" I told her a B. She quietly said, "Oh, honey, I have you as an A." It was like she was delivering some really terrible medical diagnosis! She seemed sad to have to deliver it and I wasn't thrilled to receive it. But what can you do at that point? I got the prettiest, best push-up bra I could find and went with it. You have to give yourself grace when it comes to your body—it is going to fluctuate a ton during the child-birthing years, and most likely the years after too. Take care of it but don't agonize over it. This is the perfect chance to value yourself and practice "getting the poop out of your nails"—love your body for what it can do instead of hating it for what it looks like, or doesn't look like.

Eating Well

Again, new moms, I know you are just trying to make it through the day. Your only goal is to keep everyone alive and maybe get a 20 minute nap. I get it. But you need to start healthy habits, especially if you are breastfeeding. I struggle as I write this because I am all about healthy eating but I am also all about making life manageable, not more stressful or hard. So you have to find balance. You can't allow yourself to be lazy or uninformed, but you also can't expect to cook all organic food from responsibly sustainable local farms exclusively. Without plastics or Teflon. All while drinking pure, distilled water of the rainforest. See, it can be a little overwhelming, right?

Here's my problem with the diet culture in America. It's basically information overload and everyone thinks they are an expert. Some are all about eating low calorie. Or Paleo. Some are all about being Vegan. Or trying intermittent fasting (which, by the way, is really just a fancy way of saying "skipping breakfast."). Some say to consume lots of fruit, or no fruit. No dairy. No grain. Eat for your blood type. Forgo carbs and go Keto. Is your mind spinning yet?

When I was a teenager and 20-something, it was all about eating a low-fat diet. Eat low-fat and pay no attention to the rest. Then it became about how the "calorie is king." Stay under a certain amount of calories, and nothing else really matters. Now the scary thing we hear about is the ever-evil carb. It all seems like a marketing ploy to me. Just look at the gluten-free industry. There is absolutely a group of people that need to eat gluten-free; but gluten itself is not harmful or necessary to avoid for most people. But because of marketing, we see "gluten-free!" written on all kinds of items and we're programmed to think we should avoid it too, or that we are automatically healthier by not consuming it.

I follow a lot of health-conscious gurus. They all span the spectrum of what is "healthy." One is a vegan. She eats about ten pieces of fruit a day. She is super fit. I know someone else who believes you should only eat one piece of fruit a day. She's super fit. I know Paleo enthusiasts who eat lots of good meats. Super fit. I know vegetarians—super fit. Non-grain, non-dairy folks—super fit. So, what does that mean? How can all these seemingly opposite mindsets work for so many people? Why does it seem like some "diets" are at odds with one another, yet their disciples are healthy and thriving?

I believe you have to look at what they have in common. They may all be against something, whether it be meat, carbs, or dairy; but they are all *for something* too. Each one is all about eating clean, unprocessed foods and low to no sugar. So, maybe the point is not about what to avoid eating, but more about what we *should* be eating. Whole, natural foods. Food without an ingredient list. Food that grows or moos. Instead of getting on a fad bandwagon (*cough*, Keto, *cough*), just cut out most processed food and eat like your grandparents did—the good old days when food was food and not akin to a science experiment.

Like everything else I have talked about, you do you! If you like being a vegetarian, keep it up. If eating only certain times of the day works for you, keep it up. Do what works for you, but at the same time don't fall for marketing or fads. Don't get tripped up by the inconsequential "rules" you hear about. And instead of getting confused by conflicting info, learn from what links them all—things like whole foods and regular exercise.

Do you want to live healthier but don't know where to start? Pick what you want to focus on and just do that. Six months later, add a new aspect to focus on. As you ease into it, it becomes natural and easy—not forced and unattainable. A while back I became more aware of what we were eating and the astounding amount of chemicals we were coming into contact with, and wanted to do something about it. However, the more I read and the more I researched, the more bogged down I felt. Over-information can actually be damaging if it makes you feel defeated from the get-go. So I decided to pick three areas to tackle and just focus on those. I couldn't buy 100% organic groceries, so I decided I would buy organic milk, eggs and beef. I also decided to stop buying anything with high fructose corn syrup. My third change was to stop using dryer sheets and use reusable dryer balls. Easy, maintainable choices. After that became commonplace, I chose a few other things I either wanted to add or subtract from our lives. Moms have a lot going on at once, so help yourself out and pick a few areas to work on and go from there. You will feel much more confident if you are succeeding at three simple things than if you are stressfully striving for ten.

Cooking and preparing meals seems to be at the top of the list of stress-inducing "mom jobs." I don't hate cooking, but I have definitely felt stressed out over meal planning, making sure the pantry is full of good, healthy stuff (or maybe just half-healthy stuff) and trying not to make the same three things for weeks on end. It is a big job, but someone has to do it, right? You probably feel like you are just going through the motions when it comes to preparing meals. Here's the good news: that's OK. If you go through the motions in the gym, you'll still gain muscle. Same idea here—go through the motions, build discipline, and even if you never love cooking, you will still feel success as a mom because you have provided for your family. And remember, possibly the best news of all is those kids will grow up and they can help you!

I truly encourage you to get your kids eating healthy right away. I cringe when I hear moms say their kids don't like vegetables. Well, that could be because you rarely give them any. Mash up those carrots and sweet potatoes and pretend it's as yummy as chocolate cake. Being intentional and prioritizing good nutrition will help you follow through. The more you serve it to them, the more natural it is for them to eat it. Fruits and veggies can be great snacks and are just as easy to serve as cookies and chips. Keep in mind, if your kids see you eating it, they will want to too. And please moms, don't serve your kids something different at dinner. Dinner is dinner. First, they need to eat healthy foods and learn to branch out from chicken nuggets and ketchup as a vegetable. But second, it is an extra hassle you do not need to take on. If you took the time to make a family dinner, you do not need to also make the kids something else. Family dinner is for the family. I'm trying to save you time and give you the respect you deserve.

If grocery shopping and cooking are sources of stress, you should take advantage of various programs out there. Most grocery stores have delivery options now, or online ordering where you can pick up your groceries at the store. This did not exist when my kids were little, and I tell you with certainty that I would have used that with a smile on my face. No guilt in using businesses that are designed to help you. Other companies like Blue Apron and Hello Fresh can deliver ingredients right to your door and within 30 minutes, you have a healthy, home-cooked meal on the table. Another great option is freezer cooking. Pinterest is a great resource here. You will spend a day or two in the kitchen, but will have three to four weeks of meals ready and in the freezer for when you need them. I'm taking away all the excuses to go through the closest fast food drive-thru. A little planning and effort on your part can make all the difference.

While we are on the subject of food, I have another tidbit I feel strongly about. As much as possible, eat dinner together as a family. At the dining room table. Without the TV on or cell phones out. Mike and I have done this since it was just the two of us, and we still do it now. My kids have only known that we sit and eat together, talk, and there are no phones at the table. This is a non-negotiable in our home and even though the kids may complain some, they (mostly) enjoy it and expect it too. As kids get older and more involved in extra-curricular activities, family dinners together will get fewer and farther between. To be honest, I struggle with that. I love nothing more than when everyone is home and we sit and eat and talk about our day. So even though those moments are happening less often now, I cherish the years we did have and love that my kids value it and will, hopefully, keep the practice going when they start their own families.

Please hear this. Cooking and eating can be an area that makes moms feel unworthy, less-than or full on failing. Resist it. Do your best—some days do your half-best—and move on. Don't take on unnecessary shame. If you are not a mom who home cooks every meal or who doesn't shape her kids' sandwiches into funny animal faces, that is OK. If you have no interest in learning how to puree veggies to hide in cookies, that is also OK. Don't fall into the mom guilt trap that all your meals have to be completely organic, responsibly sustained, or better yet, grown in your own backyard, and also only cost 78 cents. Do what you can, but also give yourself a break.

I'll leave you with my two most simple fall back meals I have made too many times to count. Cook up some ground beef or turkey and pour in a jar of salsa. Add some cheese. Voila! Dinner. You can put this in a tortilla and you have burritos. Put it in taco shells. Put it on tortilla chips and you have loaded nachos. You can go crazy and add some corn or black beans; really anything goes with this. Super simple and actually tasty! My second simple meal is to prepare macaroni and cheese (from a box is totally acceptable in my book), add a can of tuna and some peas, and you're done. I don't know why, but my kids have always loved this one, so on a busy night I am happy to oblige.

* * *

Thinking Well

It may seem odd to put these thoughts in this section, but hear me out. We hear a lot about mental health these days, so I am sure the concept of taking care of your mental health is not new to you. However, you may not have thought about how your mental health and motherhood are intertwined. It will do you a world of good to dive into that a bit.

There's a phenomenon I call "onslaught of opinion" the second anyone knows you're going to be a parent. How you become one doesn't seem to matter. If you are adopting you will get all the opinions, horror stories and sagas. If you are pregnant yourself, it starts even before giving birth as everyone loves to tell you how to do it, where to do it, and then give you all the gory details of their own birth stories. For your own mental health, listen politely, and then do whatever you want to do! Do not feel pressured into doing anything you and your partner aren't comfortable with. Your happiness as a new mom depends on feeling like you made the right choice for you, not for your mother, sister, friend on the other side of the aisle, and clearly not for the random stranger at the grocery store. Don't start caving to the crowd before the baby even arrives, because it only gets worse.

The opinions about childbirth, though there are many, pale in comparison to the opinions about EVERYTHING that comes after. Childcare options. Weaning. Potty-training. Discipline. Schooling choices. When to have "the talk." Dating. Decide now that you can, and should, seek out advice and guidance, but you are not beholden to any of it. You'll thrive by knowing you are parenting your way and your way only.

An example of this is the whole idea of "sleep when they sleep." This sounds like really good advice, and many people will tell you it. The first few weeks of parenting is one constant cycle of feedings, changings, and crying (for the both of you) and moms are in total survival mode. So, yes, take a nap. You need rest and your body needs to recover. But after you feel like you have the hang of things, and how long that takes is different for everyone, you have to pull yourself together. Those babies sleep a lot. Hopefully. I know this varies—my own varied a ton. When Riley was born three weeks early, he literally slept 22-23 hours a day. I had to wake him up to feed him. If someone asked me what color his eyes were, I had to think about it because I never saw them! This went on for a solid six weeks and I can't pretend I minded. Anyway, my point is I didn't need to sleep whenever he did and on top of that, I had an 18-month-old to take care of. Some advice sounds great, but isn't always practical. Sleep when they sleep is one of them. Someone has to clean the place and feed the dog at some point. I also think getting things accomplished while the kids are napping is a key to flourishing at motherhood. You get to catch up on the stuff you haven't gotten to yet, or flip through your guilty pleasure magazine and just relax.

My friend Kristen learned this principle of parenting how she thought best early on. She had just had her first baby nine weeks earlier and was attending an overnight women's conference with her baby in tow since she was breastfeeding. The morning of the second day she was up and ready when a fellow attendee approached her. She said this was her first time away overnight from her two-year-old who she was still nursing and she woke up really engorged. Would Kristen mind if she nursed her newborn a little to relieve the pressure? Her face must have registered some shock at the request because the woman assured her that she and her friends did it all the time. Thankfully Kristen did not care what anyone else thought was OK, because she was not OK with it, and politely said no. She would have beaten herself up if she had felt pressured to say yes, but definitely felt good about saying no.

* * *

The second biggest area concerning your mental health and motherhood revolves around the comparison trap. I can admit that this was a struggle for me for years. My whole childhood and teen years were filled with the idea that I wasn't good enough and never measured up. By my 20's, I must have assumed I had beaten this or wasn't affected by it so much. Then I had kids. Wow, I didn't see what was coming. I never realized that when you have kids they are truly a part of you—an extension of you, really. So all of a sudden my kids and my parenting became a whole other avenue of comparison with other moms. Was I as loving? Was I as patient? Was I too strict? Not strict enough? Was I losing the baby weight as fast as so-and-so? Did other moms sneak into the bathroom to just get ten seconds of quiet? I would have absolutely enjoyed those earlier years more if I had not worried so much about how I compared to other moms. I robbed myself, really—something I truly regret.

Parenting older kids doesn't really make this easier, but I do think getting older and maturing as a woman does. When I finally recognized this flaw in me and then worked on it, I was so glad I did, because worrying about measuring up to other moms is a whole other story these days. Should *my* kids get brand new iPhones and who should pay for them? Do I let *my* new driver drive downtown to Prom? Should I let *my* kid go somewhere if they know alcohol is easily available? Is *my* kid ready to go away to college? These are all real things I've worked through as a parent. Moms can drive themselves crazy if they are more worried about how their choices compare to other parents' choices than whether they are making the right decision for their child. Letting go of this sense of competition has given me freedom and it has made a huge difference in the amount of joy I feel as a mom.

So as you think of your overall health, remember that YOU are important. Your health, physical and mental, needs attention, especially if you want to enjoy your role as mom. You would never choose to not take your child to the doctor, you would never ignore your teen's depression, you would never allow your child to believe he is not good enough, so don't allow those things for yourself either. Think about how much worth your kids have—they are so precious and important. But you have every bit of worth as your kids, so don't devalue yourself; find freedom in taking care of you too.

* * *

Social Media

I have a love/hate relationship with social media. Some platforms I can handle more than others, some I just plain avoid (ahem, Snapchat). At the ripe old age of 45, I got to skip social media in my formative years. And boy, am I glad. I hear that same sentiment from every single one of my "mature" mom friends. None of us wish we had it growing up. So, it's funny how all young people today feel it is such an important part of life.

Don't get me wrong, I understand the appeal. It is fun to stay connected to friends, or just scroll your way through a five minute break from reality. You know the scenario—your kid dumps a bowl of spaghetti over his head, the dog steps in the mess, you scream, the dog runs... In your mom's day, getting lost in a soap opera was a good escape; now you have Instagram or just about any other social media platform you can imagine to distract you from reality.

The part I hate about social media is at the center of my concern for you and your ability to "think well," which is why I am discussing social media here. As moms, we are bombarded with messages about our parenting, our motherhood, our bodies, etc. And social media almost always exacerbates the mentality of unworthiness and not measuring up. And it doesn't get easier when your kids get older because they too will become users and see all the same images you do. Plus quite a few you won't, which is a whole other problem.

How many times have you scrolled through Facebook and seen this kind of thing: A woman exercising with her baby, clad in leggings and a sports bra, and not the faintest sign of a mom pouch. She's toned and perky and her perfect baby is happily bouncing along sweetly and for sure tantrum-free. Or possibly, the baby is strapped on her back while she does chin-ups. Chin ups?! I've literally seen that video. But you look over, well first you look down at your very prominent pouch, then you look over at your toddler and she's busy sticking her fingers up her nose. Instantly, you feel you don't measure up. And neither does your kid. Double the shame.

Or maybe you see a video with a beautiful woman. She's dressed to the nines and is carrying a briefcase. She is powerful and in charge. And you are "just a stay-at-home mom." And you allow yourself to feel less-than. Next, you see a celebrity cooking. No, she's braising. She's braising and mincing and infusing. All while swirling her wine in her fancy goblet. And you served frozen chicken nuggets. Will you go there? Will you see your efforts as nowhere near as valuable as hers? That your worth is somehow less?

Now, hear this first. If you want to be that fit mom, go after it. I'm all for it. If you want to be that high-powered exec-utive in the smart suit, fantastic. And if you enjoy mincing and braising, do it! And invite me over. But do not do anything out of shame, inferiority or insecurity. Find your passions based on what you love and are gifted at, not what social media shows you or tells you is best. And then on the flip side, do not feel bad about what you aren't passionate about or gifted at.

Personally, I am not great with numbers. I can't imagine dealing with spreadsheets and expense reports. The idea of board meetings filled with pie charts makes my heart sad. But I don't for a minute worry about this. It did take me a while to get there. I was noticing how instead of just thinking "numbers aren't my thing," I would beat myself up over it and feel that less-than mentality creep in. I felt inferior to women working in the types of roles I knew I wouldn't have excelled at. So instead of focusing on what I am good at, I let inferiority take over. None of that is a healthy way to live, let alone thrive. Now I am intentional about simply being confident in my strengths, not self-conscious about my weaknesses. I'm nowhere near "arriving" in this, but I am way closer than I was in my 20's and 30's. That is one huge advantage to growing older. It seems fair in light of gray hair and crow's feet.

We can't allow social media to make us who we are not. You will thrive as a mom, and as a woman, when you really allow yourself to just be you. With all your flaws and mistakes. You are not less of a mom when you see one of your college friends took their kids to the zoo and you haven't gone in months. You are not less of a mom when you see an old friend's kid got on the honor roll and yours is struggling academically. You are not less of a mom because a co-worker's kids have an Austrian au pair and yours go to day care. Are you getting it? It's easy to think these thoughts, but social media just seems to really bring it all to the surface. You just can't look at your life and wish Snapchat filters were real. Because no one has it all together anyway. Your friend at the zoo probably endured a toddler meltdown five minutes after the picture was posted. And maybe the honor roll kid's mom has issues with her own self-worth so she has to brag on her kids to feel better about herself. You never get the whole picture on social media.

Another way to look at it is this. If you see a beautiful woman or a great homemaker, does it make you think less of your everyday friends? If you see a handsome man, does it take away from your husband? Do cute kids on Facebook make your kids less cute? Of course not! So if what you are seeing as you scroll doesn't take away from all the people you love, why should it take away from you? If your best friend, who doesn't have a six pack, is not less worthy than the fit mom, neither are you. If your sister isn't unworthy because she can't prepare a fancy meal, neither are you.

* * *

Another reason I hate social media is simple. It's a time-sucker. How many times have you sat down for "just a breather" and 30 minutes later you have no idea what your kids are up to, but you do know what your third grade BFF had for lunch? And that your high school frenemy just got a really bad haircut. I won't lecture you on this; I am just as guilty. But do remember, your kids are watching you. Everyone complains about kids today being addicted to their phones, but I have to say, they are no more so than the adults in their lives. It's a time-waster for every age. So if you are concerned about your kids' use, or future use, start at home and consider time restraints for yourself. It's not easy to do, but possibly the solution you need.

* * *

Lastly, I also believe social media is a huge factor in the breakdown of real relationships. And when you are a mom, real relationships are vital. Now I think Facebook is great for staying up to date with old friends and Instagram is my favorite way to follow my favorite bloggers and celebrities. So, it can be good and fun. But if it keeps you from really communicating with the people in your life, that is a problem. If all you see is their highlight reel, you have no idea what is really going on in their lives, or how they may need you. And if you are only posting the positives, no one is aware of when you need help, or just someone to talk to. And you will need help on the regular. Make every effort to have real life interactions with family and friends. Don't let social media fill that void because it's just too shallow and many times, completely fake. It can't become your own personal social club—you need human interaction. I heard a speaker say once that as soon as she turns her phone off she feels lonely. Thankfully she saw that this was a problem, but it made me so sad for her. You need real, authentic people in your life, not just filtered ones.

"I keep Facebook at a safe distance, otherwise I find myself falling into the comparison pit and I can't get out. The expression "nobody's perfect" is my mantra and I believe it's true no matter what fabulousness I see on Facebook. Things aren't always what they seem and I need to stay focused on my family and not take them for granted."

Gail

"Have family 'check-in's.' Ask each other, 'How are you doing?' 'What is making you sad right now?' 'What is making you happy?' Look for what each person is going through and may need in that moment."

Kate in Pennsylvania

I hate when I'm waiting for mom to cook dinner. Then I remember that I am the mom. And I have to cook dinner.

BH&G

"Exercise is a celebration of what your body can do. Not a punishment for what you ate."

Women's Health UK

"I just want to be as fat as I thought I was in high school and as tired as I thought I was before I had kids."

@momstrosityco

CHAPTER EIGHT

FRIENDSHIP

I love friends. My friendships have been one of the biggest blessings in my life. No matter your age, I believe having a solid friend or two is so important. But during motherhood, I'd say it is essential. No one else can understand exactly what you are going through, in the same stage of life, as your buddies. So, my next piece of advice is:

Spend time with friends!

This may seem like a no-brainer for some of you. It may seem unnecessary to even discuss. If that is where you are, then I think you probably have this down. Maybe it's more for those of you that read the advice and feel sad, or lonely, or unsupported, maybe even neglected, bored, and listless. You may not have a "tribe" as is the trendy phrase right now. Or maybe since having kids your group of friends has shifted and you find yourself in a strange new place.

No matter your stage in motherhood, your friends are the ones who will help you through. Your husband, God love him, is great at many things, right? But he can't understand things the way your girlfriends can. He probably doesn't want to talk for hours about bleeding nipples and urinary incontinence. This is what we need friends for! Your friends get it, and if you got the good ones, they will stick with you through all the ups and downs of this journey.

My best friend, Kristen, and I were pregnant at the same time. She was three months ahead of me, but we got to share most of our first pregnancies together. Much to my dismay, she and her husband moved two hours away one month after she delivered. I remember talking on the phone with her a few weeks after I had Olivia and saying, "Why didn't you tell me it was going to be so hard?!" She just kind of laughed and said she didn't want to scare me. Very quickly we both realized just how much we needed each other. We literally talked on the phone every single day. It was such a lifeline for the both of us. Since we were going through it all for the first time, we could bounce questions off each other, commiserate about well, everything, and just laugh when we needed to. I'm so thankful for that friendship because it was a key piece in getting through the early years. And now, we don't talk every day anymore, but we still bounce questions off each other and commiserate, because we currently both have three teenager/twenty somethings. What we discuss now has definitely changed, but our need for each other's friendship has not.

A few years later, my other best friend from high school and college, Holly, moved back into our town. We soon got reacquainted with a mutual friend from high school, Kerry. Have you noticed how some friendships just happen so easily and seamlessly? That's how this was. We had eight kids between us, all stair-stepped in age. Thankfully our husbands all liked each other too because we had tons of family get togethers. It became another life line for me. There is such power in linking arms with others and doing life together. Holly, Kerry and I also began getting together for coffee dates whenever we could, and we would sit and laugh for hours. We talked about everything from our kids to cellulite to spirituality to our in-laws. There is something special about friends with whom you can bounce from topic to topic, serious or not, and feel a sense of security. To know that these ladies have you, they care about you, and there is no sense of competing with one another. Sadly, Kerry's family moved all the way to Florida, so our times together are few and far between. But you can bet that the three of us have one epic group text going. We still are there for each other, however we can be.

I hope that you have something like this. And hopefully your friends don't keep moving away from you! If you do not, don't agonize over it. Finding friends as an adult can be hard. It's a lot like dating really; you have to put yourself out there and hope someone likes you. Finding mom friends is so much easier when your kids are small, though. If you are setting up play dates, you are pretty much stuck with the mom. Or if your kids go to birthday parties and school functions, you will be interacting with all the other parents. This changes when your kids are teens. You may never meet their friends, let alone their friends' parents. So, let yourself be vulnerable and talk to the other moms you come into contact with. It may seem awkward at first, but it will get easier. And like I said, some friendships just come easily. You will hit it off right away and, like with dating, you may fall fast. Just find another mom and see if she and her little one would like to go to the park, or if you're feeling brave, your house. Chances are she is in desperate need of a good friend too and the two of you will enjoy spending time together. Or you may want to run the other way! That is ok too; you don't have to be besties with all the moms. I once had a neighbor I started getting to know, and it was clear early on that we were not going to be close friends. For one, she was constantly telling me how handsome Mike was (like every time I saw her) and in a lot of other important ways, we just didn't click. She also mowed her grass in stilettos, but that is neither here nor there. The point is, not every mom will be a natural fit as a friend—don't sweat it.

There is absolutely nothing wrong with keeping friendships from pre-baby days. Or having co-worker friends or single friends. I think all types of friends are important and can add value to your life. But seek out friends in the same stage of life as you too. It just helps. You need someone who understands and is going through it too. And sometimes an old friend can become a new friend that way. For me that was my sister, Misty. She and I really weren't close growing up. She was only three years older, but in a lot of ways I viewed her as a second mom. After having Olivia, she and I developed a close friendship. I learned from her the value of having someone who's gone through it already in your life. It is important to have someone to look up to and see what they did, or didn't do, to learn from. Having a mentor of sorts is critical if you want to flourish as a mother. You need someone you can ask questions, not just Google. Or maybe just vent to. You've probably noticed by now that motherhood isn't always fun. There are days when you may feel like you just can't do it and you think you are failing miserably. Having an older mom in your life to talk you through it, and hopefully share her own struggles, helps immensely. I also had a wonderful mentor, Rory, in my MOPS group. I still to this day remember something she said to us, and cling to it! She was talking about raising and training kids and she said, "It may take 18 years, but they'll get it!" I have had to remind my 17-year-old to shower and brush his teeth, so I counted on those words!

It may also be crucial to think about friendships that aren't adding value to your life. It's safe to say that becoming a mom changed you and your lifestyle quite dramatically. You may have friends that don't fit your new life, or are actually damaging to it. Some friendships can be more draining than you have the energy for. Do you have a friendship that just feels like work? Maybe you are pouring more into it than they are? Don't feel guilty about stepping back a bit. I've had to do this on occasion because I knew a certain relationship was taking its toll on me and not allowing me to mother with the same amount of joy I knew my kids deserved. Sometimes friendships are for a season and sometimes they are for life. The friendships that are for life will withstand anything; the ones that are for a season will move on and allow both parties to find their "forever people."

Keep this in mind when it comes to your friends—you don't have to agree on all the things. Our culture tells us that if we don't agree with someone, we hate them. This is simply not true. I can say with certainty that I have disagreed with every one of my friends over something regarding parenting. Whether I would have allowed something they didn't, or would not have allowed something they did, they all have differed from me at some point. And guess what? I value each one of them and think they all are fabulous moms. And if I have disagreed with them at some point, it's pretty safe to say they have also disagreed with me. We don't get tripped up on these things; we support one another and just can't worry about the differences. It brings a freedom to relationships that makes them much more enjoyable and easy.

Friendship is vital to you as a mom. Don't discount the importance and don't be closed to it; put yourself out there and remember you need to have fun too! Hanging out with friends and just laughing and having fun is actually a great way to thrive in motherhood. You will be refreshed and revived and a better mother for it.

"I wish I had a mentor/role model during all seasons of raising our children. Someone I could truly share my heart with. Another mother who had walked before me that I could share my successes, failures, fears, hopes, concerns…without being judged."

Rory

What makes things easier? Prayer and a great circle of friends to remind you that it's okay to be crazy, we're all doing the best we can."

Michelle from Georgia

Friend: Are you getting enough sleep?

Me: Sometimes when I sneeze, my eyes close. yourtango

CHAPTER NINE

MOTHERHOOD MUSINGS

This chapter is dedicated to all the phrases you are likely to start hearing once you have kids. And some are statements you may have used yourself. I've compiled a list of what I have found to be truthful and helpful, as well as the ones that rub me the wrong way. This is my way of taking these "words of wisdom" and sharing how true they've been for me as a mom.

"Don't mind the mess; the kids are making memories." Have you seen this quote? You may have it written in fancy cursive in your living room. It's not my favorite. To be sure, making a mess is an important part of kids' playing, and definitely their creativity. So at a certain level we have to embrace the glitter and homemade play-doh stuck in the carpet. On the other hand, you don't have to live in chaos for your kids to make memories. Yes, there will be messes, but they don't have to take over your house and life. I wouldn't say I am a clean freak, but I do absolutely hate clutter. So for me, if my house was a mess I didn't feel at rest. I needed it to be picked up and straightened before I could truly relax. If that resonates with you and a clean house is important, then you have every right to live in one. Make the messes, along with fantastic memories, but clean it up! You will hear not to worry about it and that they're only small for a short time, but I think there should be a balance between time spent with your kids and keeping the house in order. Ultimately though, remember this is your motherhood journey, so you do you! And if the mess doesn't bother you, then put your feet up and hope you don't step on a Lego.

"My daughter is my best friend." I'll say it up front, I cringe when I hear this. The heart behind it can be right, if your desire is to simply have a close relationship with your children in which they feel comfortable coming to you to talk. Of course, that is a worthy goal. However, there is a difference between being a support for your children and being their best friend. Maybe you think it's fine because you have only one child, or one girl. It's still dangerous for a couple reasons, and I promise this does fall in the motherhood, not parenthood, category! For one, if you treat your daughter as more of a friend, when the time comes for discipline, she may not handle it well. You are her bestie and now you want to tell her she can't stay out late? You are her girlfriend, but when dad gives a directive she doesn't like you side with him? It can create a lot of tension within the family. I also think it's a problem because you need your own friends and so does she. You cannot, and should not, talk to her about certain things. You shouldn't burden her with your marital issues or work stress. Have fun together and be silly, but don't look to her to

122

provide you with something she is not mature enough to take on. Lastly, the mother-daughter relationship will always be an unequal one. When she is a fully independent adult this can possibly change, but until then, it's definitely the case. She will always want and expect things from you, and look to you for support, but she won't be able to truly do the same for you. None of that is bad. It's the way it's supposed to be. Pursue a close relationship, by all means, but if you see her as your best friend, you will create an unhealthy, unbalanced dynamic. You can't flourish when that happens and neither can she!

"The days are long but the years are short." Here's one I do like! I heard this probably 874 times when my kids were young. I nodded and smiled and thought, *I wish these years would hurry on up!* But it isn't until your kids get into school that you realize just how true this statement is. It's especially true if you stay at home with them. This is when the phrase, "They grow up too fast!" will come into play. You see this every time you scroll through Facebook. Someone will post a picture of their child on their birthday or first day of school, no matter how old, and say, "They grow up too fast." Maybe this is just my cynical nature coming out, but there is no possible way a person can grow up *too fast!* They just grow up. And maybe we parents just have a hard time accepting it. Unless you have a five-year-old in college or your ten-year-old is getting married, it is not too fast. Let your kid grow up. If you will learn to love watching your kids mature, it won't seem so fast. It'll be fun and certainly a little sad at times, but you shouldn't let it take you by surprise. If you want to thrive in this momming business, you have to admit defeat in this department. The years do go fast and they will grow up. Determine now to not let it wreck you—that's how you counteract the angst in the quote. If you go into parenthood knowing the years fly by, but content in enjoying the ride, it doesn't have to bring you into a depression when your kids grow up.

"I gave birth naturally." So, maybe this isn't really a phrase you hear a lot, but it is a huge controversial topic. We moms have a hard time letting go of our preconceived ideas of what a "perfect birth" is. It can become a source of pride for some and a source of shame for others. Maybe you planned it to go a certain way, but because of complications, something else altogether happened. I know many moms who felt like failures after needing C-sections. This breaks my heart because becoming a mom should be joyful no matter how it happened. Some moms can be very prideful that they delivered without medication, or at home, or in a tub. If that is important to you, of course, do it. But don't put yourself up higher on the "good mom" ladder because of it. I personally had to be induced and received an epidural all three times and I don't regret it for a minute. I truly enjoyed my deliveries because I wasn't out of my mind in pain. I won't feel bad for that. I know some moms who didn't want medication during delivery, but thought nothing of drinking wine or coffee while pregnant; and then moms who wouldn't have drank alcohol or caffeine during pregnancy, but did get meds during birth. Which mom is "better" than the other? (Neither is the answer, by the way.) In the end, be glad you have a baby; that is the desired end result anyway. Think of the moms who don't get that happy ending; and please don't attach shame or guilt to however things turned out for you. Also don't award yourself an imaginary blue ribbon for doing it in a way that you see as "right." There truly is no right or wrong way to have a baby!

"No two kids are alike." Ain't this the truth! I have no idea how two kids from the same parents can be so incredibly different. Olivia came out shy. I started noticing this just a few months in. She started cooing and doing those precious little baby sounds, but only in front of Mike and I. I told everyone how cute it was, but as soon as someone else came around, she wouldn't do it. As she became a toddler she would not speak to anyone outside the family and didn't talk to her own grandpa until she was three and a half! But Riley, boy can he talk. Ironically, he was a late bloomer. He didn't talk at all until he was two, and then he never stopped! He was just as extroverted as Olivia was introverted. It was so easy taking her places because she never in a million years would have thrown a tantrum in a public place or drawn attention to herself. I thought I was just a really good mom, keeping that kid in line. Then Riley came and he didn't have those worries, and I realized it was not that I was a really good mom!

Olivia was also very maternal and loving to her dolls. One day Riley took one of her Barbie's, stared at it, then ripped her head off and threw it against the wall, laughing his own head off. Neither of my girls would have ever done that. I chalked it up to the difference between a boy and a girl, but these two weren't, and still aren't, alike! Your job is to be OK with it. You can't fit your kids into some kind of mold or expect them to think and act similarly. Nor can you put pressure on them to. I have told my kids repeatedly how special and unique they are, and how that is a great thing! God gave them each special strengths and weaknesses, and they alone get to use them. How boring would our family would be if everyone was just alike? Or in Riley's case, how loud would our house would be if we were all just like him?

"I just want more for them than I had." I know this comes from a good place. Those who grew up without much or in severe need would never wish that on their own kids. The issue I have with this is that it can be about giving your kids things in place of you. I'm all for working hard and providing a good life for you kids. But don't sacrifice *time with them* for *things for them*. Your kids want you and no toy or gadget in the world can replace that need. I want you to free yourself from feeling a need to make their childhood the one you wish you had. Do your best, work your hardest, but also just be. Be with them and be present. You won't thrive if you are always striving for more, more, more—whether that is financial or otherwise.

"Don't wear busy like a badge of honor," and **"Stop the glorification of busy."** These are so good. There is so much truth in both of those statements; I don't feel like I have much to add! It seems in our culture that we believe the busier we are, the more productive we are. So totally false. Or the busier our kids are, the better parents we are and the better humans they are. Also false. Kids need downtime, and so do you. If you want to survive motherhood well, do not say yes to everything or sign up for everything. And you don't have to let your kids do all the things either. Do you know someone like this? Maybe a friend posts day after day about all the sports her kids are in, along with school activities, church commitments, oh and dance, music lessons and karate? None of those activities are bad, and I think every kid should get to try the things that interest him or her, but not all at the same time! Mike and I decided years ago that we would only let our kids do one sport and activity at a time. With three kids, this was still three extra things for us a week. We did not want our family time overrun by busyness. It resulted in a more peaceful home and a lot less stress. Plus it was easier on us financially (that is until they started marching band—who knew that was so expensive?).

"Nobody's perfect." I hate that I even feel the need to address this one. It makes me sad that we live in a culture that promotes it and our love of celebrities and addiction to social media only perpetuates it. It is true though—nobody is perfect. As a mom, this will be true. If you want to flourish, accept it! You will not enjoy one day of motherhood if you think you have to attain some image of the perfect mom you've conjured up in your mind. By the time your kid hits 18 you will have a lifetime of screw-ups and mistakes. At some point you have to laugh about it and move on. One of my favorite screw-ups happened a few years ago. We were going through a really hard time because Mike had lost his job and I was still staying at home full-time. To say we were struggling financially is an understatement. Around Christmastime our local theater was putting on a musical and a couple of Madelyn's friends were in it, so she really wanted to go. Tickets weren't crazy expensive, but we just couldn't do it. So one day I saw in the paper that they were doing a special matinee and if you brought in a donation to the Food Pantry, you could get in free. Perfect! Madelyn was so excited to get to go and I was so happy I didn't have to say no. When we got there, I gave the lady at the front of the line our donation. She looked at me and said, "Oh, you brought...canned goods." I looked to my right and saw a giant pile of toys for Toys for Tots—the intended charity—not the Food Pantry! Oh, boy. I was horrified at my mistake, but she quietly took my canned black beans and cream of mushroom soup and added it to the pile! We got to see the play, but the whole time I was cringing at my slip-up. You can be sure Madelyn was cringing too! And I really hoped there wasn't a kid somewhere on Christmas morning unwrapping the said canned goods!

"Don't sweat the small stuff." Truer words were never spoken! The problem with this is we don't always know when stuff is the small stuff. When you have your first baby, everything seems huge. You wouldn't dream of putting a pacifier that fell on the floor back in the baby's mouth, but by the third child you may just lick it yourself and pop it right back in. Many issues you deal with at first seem hugely important, but not all are. So I don't think the advice means don't care about or don't research the best options or ideas out there. It just means don't stress about it. Don't let it consume you and definitely don't let it bring you more anxiety.

When I became a mom I was consumed with every decision being the best decision. I was constantly googling and always questioning myself. When this started to wear off

I think I was a better mom for it. You have to know when to let things go and when to relax. When she was young, Olivia went through a phase when she didn't want to sleep in her bed. No offense to you co-sleepers, but that was not our deal! So I compromised and if she came in our room in the middle of the night she could sleep on our floor. Almost every morning I'd find her all curled up beside my bed. I decided not to worry about it, knowing it was probably just a phase. Well, let me just relieve your worries, your teenager will not want to sleep anywhere near you. She absolutely grew out of it, as did all my kids' inconsequential phases. I took this same approach with Madelyn, who was a thumb sucker. I don't know if it was because she was my baby and I was over worrying about things, but I just didn't care. Truthfully, I found it pretty adorable, and also easier, because she never screamed her head off in the middle of the night trying to find that blasted binky. Unfortunately, this "phase" lasted about ten years and resulted in three years in braces, so maybe I should have cared more!

"Mom fail." This phrase really gets me going. I know it's usually used jokingly and light-hearted, but I also know that we moms take our "momming" very seriously. If we think we are failing all the time, we won't enjoy a single second of motherhood. We are setting ourselves up for literal failure. You will make mistakes, you will forget to sign that permission slip, and you will attempt to make Pinterest-worthy cupcakes, only to run to Kroger at 10 p.m. to buy truly servable ones. Don't see that as failing. View it as a normal part of life. See it as what everyone does at some point, not just you as the all-encompassing mom. Have you noticed that you never hear the phrase "dad fail?" Could it be that they don't put the same kind of insane pressure on themselves to be perfect all the time? No one expects that from them? I say let's band together and make a pact; how about we stop using the phrase and thus, erase this mindset.

I will share the biggest "fail" story I have in my repertoire. When Madelyn was a baby, and through her toddler years, she dealt with severe constipation. Like turning purple, screaming at the top of her lungs kind of constipation. We had done a slew of tests, tried different treatments, the whole nine yards. Under doctor's orders we were giving her adult Ex-lax twice a day. My first fail in this is that I called it her "chocolate," knowing the pushback I'd get if she thought of it as medicine. One weekend Mike and I went away and left the kids with grandparents. I had checked the medicine box and saw that there was plenty there and we would have plenty left over when we returned. I told the in-laws to keep it out of reach from Madelyn because she really liked eating it. When we returned that Sunday night I saw that all the Ex-lax was gone, but was assured she was only given the prescribed amount. You see where I am going with this? The next day I had all three kids at the Pediatric Dentist's office. Madelyn was off in a corner playing with toys while I thought I'd get a second to sit and relax. Not long after she came to me, rather nonchalantly, and I smelled it before I saw it. All that extra Ex-lax was doing its job and poop was just pouring out of her like a spigot. After gathering my wits, I scooped her up and raced to the bathroom. Of course I had not brought extra clothes, because she was three at this point. Paper towels were no match for the amount of poop I was dealing with, so I washed her off as best I could and had to choose whether I put poopy clothes back on her, let her go bottomless or wrap her like a mummy with paper towels. (I opted for washing out her bottoms in the sink and putting them on her wet, in case you were wondering.) Here comes the worst part. As I exited the bathroom I noticed most of the staff staring at me and I looked to my side to see THE DENTIST on his hands and knees scrubbing the carpet where Maddie, and her eruption, had been. I quickly offered to take over but he wouldn't even acknowledge me standing there. It was so awkward! He finished up and a little while later I was called over to where Olivia and Riley were getting their cleanings. The dentist gave me a death stare and said, "Sorry for the long wait, but I had quite the mess to clean up." I was so taken aback and responded with, "I told you I would clean it up!" And really, why was he doing it and not one of his employees? Needless to say, we never went back to that office and I am sure they were happy to lose us. Moral of that story is don't refer to medicine as chocolate and don't expect caregivers to always follow your instructions!

"Mom of the Year." This phrase is very close to "mom fail." How many times have you felt terrible about something you did and told on yourself, saying, "I'm like Mom of the Year over here!" I know I've said it. It's fine to tell funny stories about parenting—I've told you many—but it's not helpful to put this expectation on yourself that you aren't going to make little mistakes, or even big ones, for that matter. And when you do, please strive to have the right perspective and move past it.

When Olivia was in third grade she got glasses. Now, I have to tell you that she had mentioned to me repeatedly that she wasn't able to see well. I shrugged it off and didn't take it too seriously, probably because I have never had vision problems. But I finally took her to the eye doctor and unsurprisingly, she needed glasses. In fact the doctor's words were, "She has the eyesight of a 70-year-old man." I had no idea how bad her eyesight was, and neither did she, because getting glasses was life-changing for her. She was in shock that she could see individual blades of grass and not just a sea of green. I felt so horrible about not taking care of it sooner, and every time I told the story, I always added, "I guess I'm Mom of the Year." Is this harmless self-deprecation, or just our way of admitting we think we suck...but in a funny way? I don't know, but I think we should examine whether or not it's healthy to use that term. My vote is we don't.

"Dad's babysitting." No he isn't, he's parenting. Same with "Daddy diaper duty." Would you ever think to say "Mommy diaper duty?" It's stupid and insulting to fathers. Let's stop saying this one too.

"Pick your battles." This phrase can work in a lot of areas, but I think it works perfectly in the motherhood realm. Picking your battles starts early, maybe even day one. I think it's kind of a sliding scale because the battles you choose to pick when your kids are small seem huge, but once they grow up... not so much. Your toddler begging to wear a Spiderman costume, princess tiara and rain boots to pre-school might seem like a big one, and maybe you decided to give in on that one (do give in on that one), but that same kid will grow up and in junior high be asked to a dance and want to wear a dress you find a bit too revealing. Should you give in on that? I bet you wish she wanted to wear the Spiderman costume now, right? My job isn't to tell you how to handle the dress situation, just to remember that whatever you decide, each and every choice is up to you.

Picking my battles has never been too big of an issue for me because many times, I just don't care. My kids used to tattle on each other (who am I kidding, they still do!) over pretty insignificant things. My feeling, and sometimes actual response, was, "I can't care." I left many things to them to sort out together; I realized pretty early on that I have too many things that actually matter than to care whether one of my daughters borrowed their brother's ear buds without asking. Or whose turn it is to pick the movie. And even though I like a tidy house, I don't "pick the battle" of my kid's bedrooms being clean. They aren't complete disasters, but they almost never make their beds and always have laundry piling up. For me, I need the downstairs areas straightened; I just can't care about their bedrooms too. So I leave that battle alone. This will look different for everyone, but if living peacefully makes you a better mom, do what it takes to see that happen.

"It takes a village." This phrase is another one that I feel two-sided on. I do believe it's true. Parenting is a lot of work and takes a lot of people pitching in. There is no question that your family, schools, churches, and community will all take part in shaping your kids' lives. Also, I've been adamant about asking for help, and not seeing help as an indictment of your parenting skills. I want all moms to feel supported and strengthened by all the other people in their circles. My friend Kerry realized that taking turns driving kids around is a primary way she participates in a "village." She says when it's her turn to drive she gets a great peek into the social world of her daughter and her friends, and when another mom drives, her daughter gets to know another caring adult. And that they can all keep tabs on the kids. I love that practical way of looking at it.

But I also want you to see the flip side. While it takes a village, you don't need the village's approval. There are so many questions that come as a parent, I just want you to thrive in knowing that you are equipped for this and you can do this. Any child God put you in charge of, He trusts you to thrive as their mom. So if searching Google gives you peace of mind about something, then by all means, knock yourself out. But also know that sometimes all the village you need is your very own mothering instincts.

"Happy wife, happy life." I saved the worst for last! I absolutely hate this phrase. Similar to this phrase is "If momma ain't happy, ain't nobody happy." It paints women as the domineering, my-way-goes, mom bully and it paints men as weak pushovers. Should your husband go out of his way to show you love? Absolutely. But should he do it because you will make his life crappy if he doesn't? I sure hope you wouldn't. Do you like women being painted as the shrew that always has to have the upper hand and be catered to? And shouldn't you be going out of your way for him? You will thrive as a wife, and then in turn as a mom, when you banish this line of thinking. Your husband does not exist just to make your life happy.

"I'm really thankful for my village. On good days I am thankful I have people to share my stories with— stories of success or funny things they say. On busy days, I'm thankful I have people to help chauffeur or babysit. And on hard days, I'm thankful for those who have gone before me, who have been where I've been and who listen as I pour my heart out. I'm thankful for those who care and pray and I'm incredibly thankful I don't have to go it alone."

Holly in Ohio

I'm going to write a parenting book called, "Fine. Whatever. Go ahead."

@MotherPlaylist

CHAPTER TEN

SPIRITUAL HEALTH

I haven't said a lot about spirituality up to this point. That's been very intentional. I didn't want to exclude anyone who needs a book like this; I want to appeal to every mom out there. But because my heart is to meet everyone where they are and help every mom thrive, I can't leave it out either. Being a Christian is central to who I am, and it's the only way I have been able to be a good parent.

I was raised in a Christian home and went to church my whole life but it was in college that my faith became my own. I pursued my relationship with Jesus, not because my parents were making me, but because I wanted to, which in turn made my faith deeper and much more personal. After becoming a mom, it was my everything. Becoming a parent, as you have probably noticed, is scary and hard. Having a solid faith was paramount for me. But it didn't make things perfect. And it certainly didn't mean that I wouldn't make mistakes or have fears.

I will tell you what it did mean, though. When a person decides to follow Christ, a lot of things take place. I can't even begin to list it all here because the list is too lengthy. Most people think it just means that they get to go to heaven when they die, which is certainly true. However, if that is all you think salvation is for, or all you want from it, you're missing out. John 1:12-13 says, "But as many as received Him, to them He gave the right to become children of God, even to those who believe in His name, who were born, not of blood nor of the will of the flesh not the will of man, but of God." Now, that might seem like a mouthful there, so let's focus on this: Have you ever considered what it means to be "children of God?"

Do you ever think about the babies celebrities adopt? They, by nothing of their own doing, get placed into the home of someone fantastically rich and famous and live a dramatically different life than they may otherwise have had. Now, the metaphor breaks down because we all know that being rich and famous doesn't guarantee a happy life. But think about how this works with us—God adopts us as His child, not because of anything we have or haven't done, and loves us unconditionally. We are now given a dramatically different life than we may otherwise have had. We can go to Him as a father, with all the rights of His offspring. He actually wants us to.

There are literally dozens of "positional truths" that are true of you if you place your faith in Christ. I encourage you to do a study and find out more, because it will be life changing for you—which will be mom-life- changing for you as well.

But hear what 2 Corinthians 5:17 says about someone who becomes a Christian: "Therefore if anyone is in Christ, he is a new creature; the old things passed away; behold, new things have come." If you have made the choice to follow Jesus, you are a new creature. Your past doesn't matter, nor does it disqualify you from knowing Him. You can have freedom from past hurts and hope for the future. I would love for that truth to free you as you go through your motherhood journey. He has, or will, make you new—how do you think that could affect your mothering?

You may feel like you didn't have good examples of solid parenting, so you won't be a good mom yourself. Maybe you are a child of divorce, so in the back of your mind you are always expecting that to be your marriage's fate. Perhaps you lived wild and crazy during your teens and think there is no way you are "good enough" to be loved by God. These are all lies. As the Scripture says, you are a new creation—nothing needs to hold you back anymore. Furthermore, nothing is a deal-breaker to God—He has already accepted you. Even better—He loves you. These "new things" that "have come" can give you a new way of looking at yourself. You are no longer a child of a neglectful parent or a child of a broken home—you are a Child of God. Brand new and not tied to the past.

The Holy Spirit

If someone is a Christian, they have an automatic ace in the hole. They have a Comforter, an Advocate, and a Counselor. In the book of John, Jesus tells his followers that He's leaving. He knows He's about to be crucified and though He will be resurrected, He will not be sticking around Earth. The thing is that Jesus, though fully God, was also just a human man while on Earth. He couldn't be everywhere, and He couldn't be with each of His followers all the time. But He knew someone who could. So He promised that though He was leaving, something even better was coming—the Holy Spirit, who He refers to as "an Advocate"—someone who can be everywhere at all times, available at all times and full of help for believers.

The Holy Spirit is available to us now too! Moms, that's a game-changer. Do you go through the day feeling unsure, discouraged or angry? Parenting brings out all those feelings and more. But you may not have thought about the fact that you have access to a Helper. If you will tap into His power, everything in life, including parenting, will not seem so daunting. Romans 8:26 says the Spirit helps us in our weakness. I don't know about you, but I feel weak on the regular, and I am desperate for help. No matter what stage of parenting you are in, I am confident that you'd like it too.

* * *

How do we live this out?

So, what does all this look like on a tangible level? Prayer is a great starting point.

Praying daily is key. I definitely skip days or even fall asleep during prayer, so please don't get an unrealistic idea. I'm not perfect at it at all but I see it as foundational to who I am, so it's foundational to me as a mom. I pray daily to be filled with the Holy Spirit. I don't believe He leaves us, but I pray daily for a fresh infilling. Because, let's be real, how many times have you fallen into bed at night feeling completely drained and empty? Then you wake up, most likely earlier than you would like, and have to start right back at it. I know I need to feel like I have a fresh infusion of supernatural power. It's like putting gas in your car or getting a caffeine fix. It's a supercharge.

I literally pray for the Holy Spirit to fill me and I ask that the fruit of the Spirit will be evident in my life that day. The fruits, according to Galatians 5:22, are love, joy, peace, patience, kindness, goodness, faithfulness, gentleness and self-control. Any of those sound like something you need? I need all nine. Sometimes before noon I need all nine! The part I love and find so comforting is that these fruits aren't dependent on me; they aren't in response to what I excel at or how I am feeling that day. They are of the Holy Spirit. So it doesn't matter if I am tired, cranky or PMS-ing. In spite of myself, I have access to all of them—because of Him. I find this fact a huge, gracious, and loving act from God. I don't have to have it in me because I have *Him* in me. He provides it for me. So as a tired or frustrated mom, rely on His strength, His power and His fruit. You can't do it on your own, but the awesome thing is you don't have to.

A verse that I love, and is so applicable to moms, is Romans 15:13. It says, "May the God of hope fill you with all joy and peace as you trust in Him, so that you may overflow with hope by the power of the Holy Spirit." I love the cause and effect of this prayer. God fills us with joy and peace *so that* we overflow with hope. All we have to do is trust in Him. Now that can be hard to do at times, but I completely believe it's a learned behavior. You may not be there yet, but the more you trust and see Him working in your life, the easier it is to keep trusting.

I believe the "hope" of this verse is multi-dimensional. Primarily, I believe hope is for our redemption from sin and the assurance of our eternal security. But for day-to-day, year-to-year earthly life, we have joy and peace and hope now as well. Do you need joy in the midst of all-night-long feedings, and when the baby is crying, for seemingly no reason? Do you need peace about whether to expand your family? Maybe you have a child with special needs and hope for the future is what you are clinging to? I don't know where you are or what battle you're in, but I do know that the God of hope is waiting for you to trust in Him. Thriving in motherhood absolutely hinges on this.

Prayer is just communicating with God. There is absolutely nothing we can't take to Him, and He wants us to come to Him with our needs. One of my favorite verses is Philippians 4:6, "Do not be anxious about anything, but in every situation, by prayer and petition, with thanksgiving, present your requests to God." Read the verse that comes after for a truly great promise. But first, see that God wants us to present our requests. When it's 3:00 a.m. and the baby will not go to sleep, pray. When you have to drop your baby off at kindergarten and you just don't know how you'll cope, pray. When your third grader is being bullied and you want to find that little... pray. There is literally nothing we can't bring before Him.

I have personally prayed for tons of things concerning my kids. It doesn't mean that God is my personal genie in a bottle, granting my every wish. But He always brings comfort and has absolutely answered many prayers. When Madelyn was born, Riley was only two and a half and still needed a lot of sleep himself. She was not easy to get to sleep, sometimes taking hours, and I didn't want to let her cry because it would keep Riley and Olivia up. The first months were super stressful because all she wanted was to throw midnight dance parties while the rest of us just wanted to sleep already. I was completely exhausted and at my wits end. So, I simply prayed. I asked God to make her a great sleeper—that she would go down peacefully and allow us to all sleep well. I even decided to fast, because man, I was serious about this. It may seem like a small issue, but at the time it felt huge to me. I only fasted chocolate because I was breastfeeding and I still needed calories, but certainly didn't need *chocolate calories*—my calories of choice. After my pre-designated days were up, it was like a light switch was flipped. She went down like a dream and never cried once. Ever. There is no other way to explain that than to say God certainly intervened for us. It was small in the grand scheme of things, but felt like a sweet hug from Him. It proved to me that nothing is too small and nothing is unimportant to Him.

Another answer to prayer concerned Madelyn again. It was December and during the time I mentioned Mike had lost his job (actually the following December from the canned goods story, if that tells you how horribly long that struggle was) and money was even tighter. Maddie was obsessed with the ballet The Nutcracker, and had wanted to go see it for a few years. Obviously, that year it was completely out of the question. One day a local radio station had a drawing to win two tickets. We entered and I told her we were going to pray that she would win those tickets so we could attend. Well, guess what? We didn't win. I was so disappointed—I had wanted her to see that God answers our prayers, plus I wanted her to be able to see the show! A few days later I went to get our mail and in our mailbox was an envelope—*with four Nutcracker tickets* for that very weekend. I was flabbergasted. It did not say who they were from; the envelope only contained the tickets along with a generous Target gift card. After some investigating, it turned out they were from the church we were attending. They had no idea of Madelyn's desire, they were just aware of our situation and wanted to bless us with something fun. But God knew, and I loved that He proved He didn't need a radio station to give us two tickets; He could give us four in an even grander way. What a joy it was to present those tickets to her and see the absolute excitement on her sweet little face. And, in case you are wondering how our family of five handled the four ticket situation—thankfully neither Olivia or Riley cared to go, but my nephew wanted to see it too, so the four tickets turned out perfectly.

The best part of prayer isn't getting the answers we want. I mentioned the verse in Philippians that I love about "presenting our requests to God." The verse that comes after is one of the best promises you can find in the Bible. It says, after praying, "The peace of God, which transcends all understanding, will guard your hearts and your minds in Christ Jesus." It will guard my heart and mind? Like not let the worries in? Not let my anxiousness grow into full-on panic attacks? Yes. I also love the phrase, "which transcends all understanding." You won't understand why you can be at peace when you just received a scary diagnosis, or why you aren't falling apart when your teen tells you they got suspended. If you put in the work and are petitioning the God of the universe, He promises to send you His peace. It doesn't even have to be *your* peace, it's His, and He loves to share.

* * *

Another prime way to "trust in Him" is by doing simple, daily choices. I mentioned prayer, which I think is probably number one on the list. I also believe strongly in Bible reading. The amazing thing about the Bible is that you will never run out of new and interesting truths. No matter how many times you read it, there is always a new way God can use it to speak to you. If you haven't ever read it, or have tried and found it intimidating or even boring, don't worry about it. Start fresh and let it be a tool in your life. The most basic advice is to start in the New Testament and go from there. People tend to think of the Bible as an outdated book of do's and don'ts. I don't find this to be the case at all; for me, it's a book full of promises. My favorite books are Ephesians and Philippians. Start reading and figure out which ones are yours. If you don't have a Bible, there are great apps out there. You Version is my favorite—you can read a chapter while in the car pool lane, or a quick scripture or devotional while feeding your baby. Don't feel as though you have to commit to hours of reading each day. Start with one verse if that is all you can do and go from there. I do highly recommend a Bible reading plan. It's so helpful when you don't know where to start or what to read next. Plus it will keep you on track.

Another dimension to Bible reading is Scripture memorization. I will be completely honest and say that I am not good at this, but it is something I am working at for sure. Having certain Scriptures memorized will help you more than you know. It can be like movie lines or song lyrics popping into your mind at times. Scripture can become the same—automatic and instinctual. When you are going through a rough moment or even a rough season, certain verses can be just the truth you need to get through.

One of my favorites is pretty commonly known, Philippians 4:13: "I can do all things through Him who gives me strength." The verses leading up to it are pretty important for reference. The author, Paul, is talking here about how he has learned contentment. He says he knows what it's like to be in need, and if you know anything about Paul, he went through his share of hardships. He'd been imprisoned, beaten, ship-wrecked and stoned. More than once. So, for him to say he's learned how to be content, and can "do all things," after all of that, is eye-opening. The key section of this verse though is not, "I can do all things," as much as it is, "through Him who gives me strength." That is the part I want you to find hope in. Next time your baby spits up all over your newly ironed shirt, or your toddler is having an epic meltdown in the grocery store, remember through Him giving you strength, you can do this. Commit the verse to memory and as it becomes natural, let it transform you.

* * *

Another way to grow in your spiritual life is pretty obvi-ous—go to church. This can be easier said than done, I know. But sometimes it takes a little church shopping to find the right fit for your family. If you have never gone, or haven't in a while, give it a try. There are so many churches out there that are family oriented, contemporary and even fun. This can be where you find a tremendous support system. Plus, they have nurseries! You can let your little ones be loved on and enter-tained by others while you enjoy an hour of calm. So, even if your reason is self-serving, if it gets you there, I'm all for it. The church we attended when we were first having kids had an amazing ministry. They would provide dinners for two whole weeks for new parents. Two weeks! It was such a blessing to us, and we felt loved and cared for by it. So, yeah, free meals.

An extra blessing to going to church? Your kids get to go too. Do not discount how significant this can be for them, no matter how young. Whether they are babies being rocked in the nursery or toddlers singing "Jesus Loves Me," they are getting a foundation into who He is and what living for Him looks like. Kids' spiritual formation is primarily on the parents, but church attendance plays an enormous role too. If you feel like you personally aren't at a place to adequately pour into your kid's spiritual lives, then providing them an avenue that does will absolutely increase your happiness as a mom.

Many churches will have small groups. These can be so life-giving. Mike and I have been involved with many groups over the years and they have been a great source for spiritual growth. It can be intimidating to open yourself up to new people, but don't let that stop you. Seek out groups that have families with kids—it's great to have that comradery. People going through similar circumstances have a special connection; there's nothing like going through potty-training together to really form a bond, right? On the other hand, don't underestimate the importance of having older, seasoned folks in your life too. You never know, they just might be itching to hold that squirmy baby and give you a break. No matter who is in the group, it will give you a chance to link arms with others and do life together. That feeling of community can play a huge role in how much satisfaction you are feeling spiritually, which will leak into the other areas of your life as well.

* * *

Lastly, if you want to grow spiritually, fill your mind with godly things. The more godliness you consume, the more it exudes out of you. This can come in a lot of forms, and can vary for different people. For me, worship music is key. I am not a fan of Christian music per se, but I do love good worship music. There is a difference! I love to have good worship on while I go about my day—it centers me and puts my mind on Him and not myself. I see it almost as prayer—I am singing words of love to God that I probably wouldn't say. But as I worship, or even just listen to others worshipping, I feel closer to Him and it fills me with peace.

I also love Christian podcasts. I listen the most while I am getting ready in the morning, or while out and about doing errands. There is a wealth of opportunity here—literally thousands to pick from. Whether you are newer in your faith or have been at it your whole life, there is something for you. If you have a favorite pastor or writer, chances are there will be podcasts featuring them. I have a few favorites right now that feed me spiritually, but also make me laugh—something I can get behind. Take a peek at what's out there and you will most definitely find something you love too.

Since you are reading this, I'm going to take a guess that you like to read. Me too! I am a huge reader; I go into bookstores and literally get a jolt of excitement at all the beautiful books on the shelves. Oh, and the smell, I just love it. Like music and podcasts, books can be key in aiding your spiritual growth. The Bible will always be the number one way to learn about God, but books written by normal, everyday people can be extremely helpful too. I have so many authors I love, so go to a bookstore or the library and get a feel for who can speak into your life. You won't be sorry.

* * *

Grace

Oh moms, here's the best news I can give you. Along with salvation, the greatest gift we are given comes in the form of grace. The word grace is used around 200 times in the Bible. It's all about how we have been given a gift, not based on anything we have done, but based on what Jesus did on the cross. So primarily grace is all about how we have forgiveness from sin and are seen as right and holy before God.

But it doesn't stop there. Hebrews 4:16 says, "Let us approach God's throne of grace with confidence, so that we may receive mercy and find grace to help us in our time of need." There is so much good stuff packed into that sentence. First, the whole idea of a throne invokes authority. God is very much in command, however; His rule is one marked by grace, not condemnation. He has come to bring life, not condemn it. I love that it says to approach God *with confidence* (some translations say with boldness) that in itself is full of grace—we don't need to be afraid to come to Him, nor do we need to think we are undeserving or that He doesn't care what we are going through. We are literally given the liberty to not just address the God of the universe, but to have the audacity to believe He cares about our prayers.

What I really love comes next. We are told to approach God so that we will receive mercy and *find grace*. The concept of finding grace paints such a vivid picture. It reminds me of little kids hunting for Easter eggs. You can picture the scene—a slew of children armed with plastic baskets, thrown in a field while their parents holler at them to "look over there!" You see, parents know exactly where the eggs are. Usually they are in sight plain as day, but kids are running wild, all willy-nilly, looking everywhere but the spots the eggs are in. Then a child sees it, squeals with delight and scoops up that egg for himself. What does he do next? Immediately pops it right open to see what the treasure is inside. Like an Easter egg hiding in plain sight, God provides the grace; you don't have to run in every direction looking for it. He already has it for you, so scoop it up!

The second part of the verse is important too. It says we will receive mercy and find grace "in our time of need." The Bible doesn't promise a problem-free life. It is saying right there that you *will* have a time of need. I'm guessing this is the part of the verse you are able to wrap your mind around. But if the second part of the verse (having a time of need) is true, the first part (God giving us grace) is as well. Think on that so it becomes real to you. I just love that God, in His infinite wisdom, provided all of us what we would need to get through.

Have you made decisions you regret? Do you think you are less than adequate as a mom? Do you feel agony about making hard choices? Those emotions may not go away, but what can overshadow them is the grace of God. If you trust in Him, He sees you as His child. Blameless. Holy. An heir. That should change the way you think. It doesn't mean you won't make more wrong decisions or feel like the world's worst mom on occasion, but it does mean that He sees you as qualified and more than enough. So there is no reason to beat yourself up or feel inferior. Let yourself receive that grace and live in it instead.

So the next time you think you are "Mom of the Year" (even though we aren't using that phrase anymore, right?) remember that you live under grace, not condemnation. And even if your Instagram feed shows way more capable moms that never yell at their kids, you are under grace. You are under grace when you snap at your husband, complain about your boss, and feed your toddler a Pop-tart for breakfast. Isn't that freeing? It should be. If it doesn't feel freeing to you, you are probably not truly grasping the magnitude of it. Do me a favor and read the verse again, and then again and again. Read it until you can recite it as well as your favorite teenage anthem. Get it into your mind and your heart until it becomes real. Do you think you would live differently by believing God's grace is a free gift available to you today? I sure hope so.

* * *

I will leave you with one more verse. Psalm 91:2 says, "I will say of the Lord, 'He is my refuge and my fortress, my God, in whom I trust.'" This is a good one to read and see if it resonates with you. If it doesn't, you probably don't look to God in this capacity. You aren't seeing Him as your refuge or your help. Certainly not one you're trusting in. I went through a season like that. The best word I can come up with is floundering. I felt like I was just going through the motions and I wasn't feeling content or joyful in any aspect of life. I started saying a sentence—it was a prayer, but it also felt like a proclamation of sorts too. All day long, whenever I felt this way I would simply say, "God, help me to love you." I knew my feelings were in direct proportion to how much effort I was putting into my spiritual health. At that point I was putting in very little. And I'll be honest and say that even though I believed in my head, I wasn't feeling it in my heart. Mothering felt so overwhelming and taxing that I didn't put my spiritual needs first. But the more I prayed that prayer, the more I felt drawn to Him. I actually wanted to pray, I wanted to learn, I wanted to feel close to Him. In turn, I saw Him as my refuge and fortress. It didn't mean that life became easy, but it did mean that I felt a connection that I had lost sight of. Going through it all alone is not sustainable or easy, but going through it with Him does make a world of difference. Your motherhood journey will reap the benefit and you will never, ever be sorry.

"Life with God is not immunity from difficulties, but
peace within difficulties."

C.S. Lewis

ACKNOWLEDGEMENTS

Writing this book was one of the hardest things I've ever done. It was something I have always wanted to do but I was always too busy, too scared, and probably a bit too undisciplined. When I finally jumped in I felt something I hadn't expected—utter terror. Putting myself, and my family, "out there" left me feeling way more vulnerable than I had anticipated. Should I really tell *that* story? What would people say about *that* advice? Can I really use *poop* in my title?! I almost threw in the towel on more than one occasion but ultimately didn't—thanks to a crew of people I am so grateful for.

Holly, Kristen, and Kerry, you three were the very best cheering section. Each of you listened as I lamented, complained, and peppered you with questions. I am truly grateful for your friendship. Kate, Jill, and all my friends that shared their stories and advice, thank you.

My sister, Misty, you have been an anchor for me. I appreciate how dependable, trustworthy, and constant you are in my life—and for basically forcing me to use poop in the title. Thank you to my mother-in-law, Peggy, for cheering me on. Your encouragement means so much to me.

Christen Johnson, your expertise was immeasurable. Your editing help not only corrected my excessive comma problem, it simply made the whole manuscript better. Your ideas and thoughts elevated it to another level, so thank you. Stacey Thacker, thank you for getting me started on this journey and helping me find my way. You are a great guide.

Olivia, Riley and Madelyn, thank you for allowing me to share embarrassing stories and talk about your poop. You guys have been super supportive and I appreciate it so much. Being your mom has been the biggest blessing of my life.

Mike, thank you for making me follow through. Your New Year's goal for me to "just have an outline done by your birthday" was a small push, but it's what got me to actually start. I am thankful for your belief in me and your steadiness in this process. Thank you for loving me.

And as cliché as it may be, I have to thank God. His "still, small voice" has been a guide to me my whole life. But in this case, I heard his voice loud and clear in multiple ways. He knew I needed that, and it worked. Thankful isn't a big enough word to express how I feel when it comes to how He has helped me through this process—not just with the writing of the book, but with the 20 years of material that came before it.